EDITORIAL
MICHAEL WINTERBOTTOM
michael.winterbottom@totalcatholic.com

DESIGN
SUE ASHTON
sue.ashton@totalcatholic.com

ADVERTISING
MARY KELLY
0161 488 1736
mary.kelly@totalcatholic.net

CIRCULATION
ANDREA BLACK
0161 488 1716
andrea.black@totalcatholic.net

PRINTING
BUXTON PRESS LIMITED
PALACE ROAD
BUXTON
DERBYSHIRE
S17 6AE

PUBLISHER
GABRIEL COMMUNICATIONS
FOURTH FLOOR
LANDMARK HOUSE
STATION ROAD
CHEADLE HULME
CHESHIRE
SK8 7JH
0161 488 1700

"I WILL GIVE UNTO THEE THE KEYS OF THE KINGDOM OF HEAVEN; AND WHATSOEVER THOU SHALT BIND ON EARTH SHALL BE BOUND IN HEAVEN; WHOSOEVER THOU SHALT LOOSE ON EARTH SHALL BE LOOSED IN HEAVEN."

Jesus to Peter. Matthew 16:19

Following on from the crucifixion of Jesus, it was the Apostle and Galilian fisherman Peter who assumed the leadership of the infant Church. As the Church developed over the centuries, after the martyrdom of St. Peter, a structured hierarchy began to be developed and under the leadership of succeeding popes the church flourished becoming as much a temporal sovereign power as a spiritual one. It has never in its history been a spectator to world events but has throughout been a major player and a formative power in an evolving world.

Before the unification of Italy in 1861, the Pope was the ruler (in a civil as well as a spiritual sense) of a number of territories on the Italian peninsular. These territories known as the Papal States eventually saw the pope as Italy's most powerful secular ruler. However as Italy gradually unified under the House of Savoy the Papal States were gradually conquered and formally annexed to the new Kingdom, until finally in 1861, Rome itself was declared the capital of the new state, the Papal Palace, the Quirinal, became the new royal palace of the King of Italy and the furious pontiff withdrew within the walls of the Vatican itself.

So the Papacy began the 20th century stripped of political power and with the Pope a self proclaimed prisoner inside the Vatican. Fortunately however this loss of temporal power freed the papacy to focus on the moral and spiritual mission of the Church throughout two World Wars and through all the social and political upheavals of the 20th century. Under the leadership of the popes the papacy throughout the 20th century continued to provide leadership and guidance to the Universal Church of believers across the globe. 900 million human beings all looking towards their Holy Father for both spiritual and moral guidance.

In the following pages, through words and images, I have attempted to present not just simple biographies of these nine famous men, but rather to give a glimpse into their world and their personalities, as they grappled with the century in which they lived and attempted to discern the will of the master whom they all served.

Michael Winterbottom

08 Pope Leo XIII
Pontificate February 20, 1878 to July 20, 1903

Pope Leo XIII (February 20, 1878 to July 20, 1903), was the pope who's reign spanned two centuries. His papacy saw enormous changes in European society, as socialism became a dominant political force, reflecting a growth in disillusionment among the working class, with whom Leo tried to build bridges and stem the flow of anti-clerical rhetoric that was resulting from their increasing poverty.

12 Pope St. Pius X
Pontificate August 4, 1903 to August 20, 1914

A fierce critic of modernism and suppporter of Thomas Aquinas, **Pope St. Pius X** (August 4, 1903 to August 20, 1914) reinvigorated the faith in the face of increasing indifference to the teachings of the Church.

16 Pope Benedict XV
Pontificate September 3, 1914 to January 22, 1922

The horror of the First World War cast a long shadow over the papacy of **Pope Benedict XV** (September 3, 1914 to January 22, 1922), and his failure to bring about a peaceful settlement to the conflict left him bitterly disappointed.

20 Pope Pius XI
Pontificate February 6, 1922 to February 10, 1939

The astonishing rise from the humble position of Vatican librarian to the papacy of **Pope Pius XI** (February 6, 1922 to February 10, 1939), highlights an astonishing intellect and thirst for widening the Church's appeal.

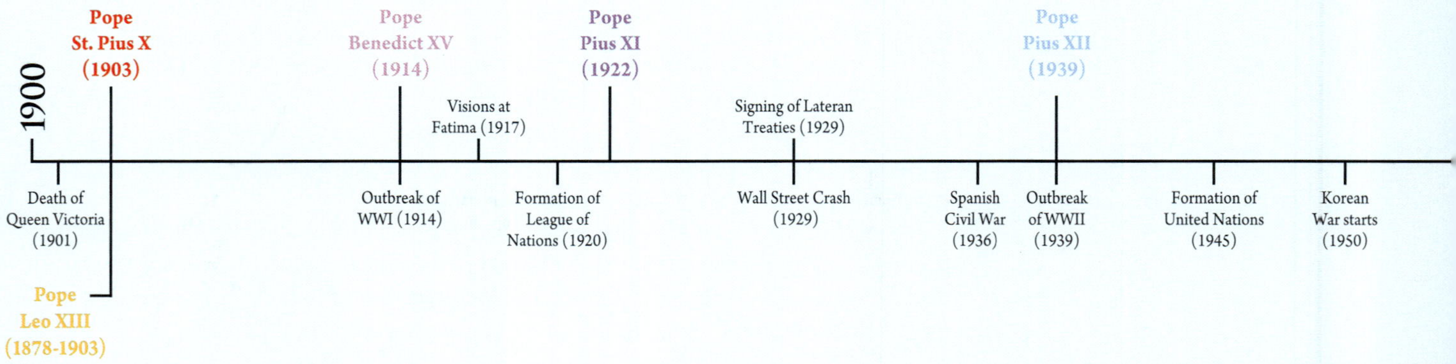

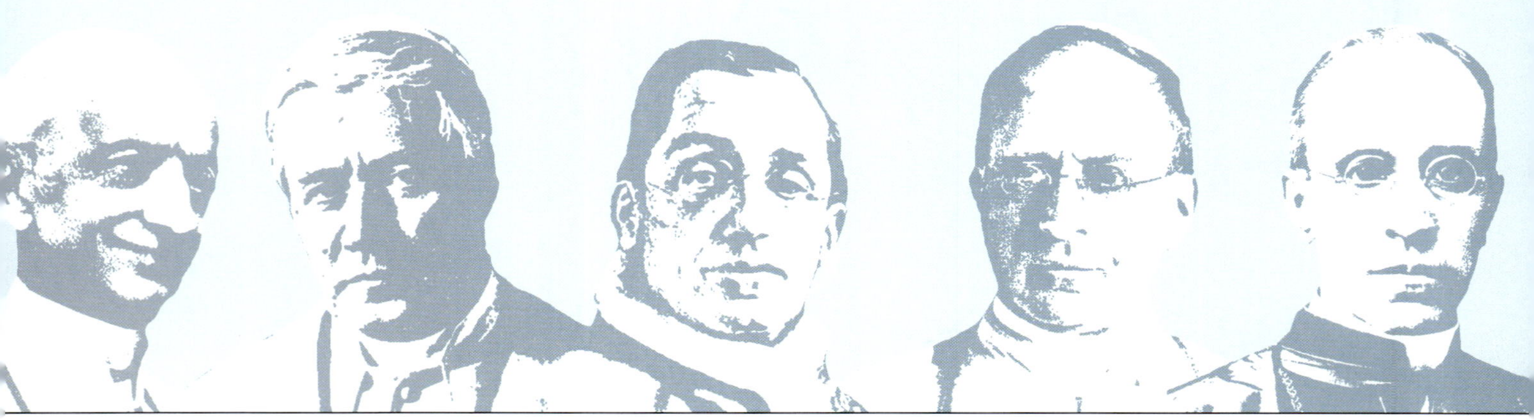

28 Pope Venerable Pius XII

PONTIFICATE MARCH 2, 1939 TO OCTOBER 9, 1958

History is now starting to re-evaluate the record of **Pope Venerable Pius XII** (March 2, 1939 to October 9, 1958), the man who guided the Church through the fear and and horror of World War II.

42 Pope Blessed John XXIII

PONTIFICATE OCTOBER 28, 1958 TO JUNE 3, 1963

Though Pope for just five years, **Pope Blessed John XXIII** (October 28, 1958 to June 3, 1963) is fondly remembered as a man who radiated the peace of the Lord to all who met him.

54 Pope Paul VI

PONTIFICATE JUNE 21, 1963 TO AUGUST 6, 1978

No Pope has overseen as much change in the ways of the Church as **Pope Paul VI** (June 21, 1963 to August 6, 1978), the man known as the 'first modern Pope.'

62 Pope John Paul I

PONTIFICATE AUGUST 26, 1978 TO SEPTEMBER 28, 1978

For just 33 days, **Pope John Paul I** (August 26 to September 28, 1978), led the Catholic Church... but in that short time he made a lasting impression on all who met him.

64 Pope John Paul II

PONTIFICATE OCTOBER 16, 1978 TO APRIL 2, 2005

Few people have touched as many lives – and hearts – as **Pope John Paul II** (October 16, 1978 to April 2, 2005) did during his 27 years as pontiff, and his gift for communicating easily with people from all faiths and none turned him into a global statesman of world renown.

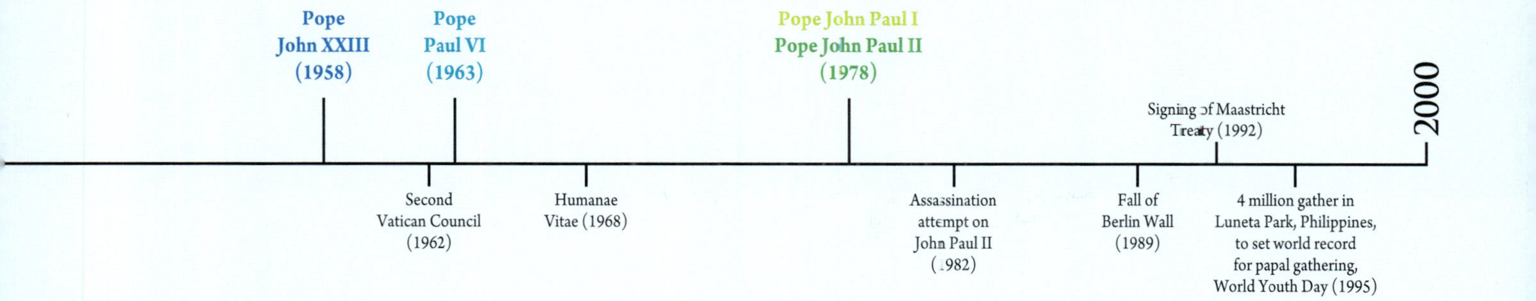

THE ROMAN CURIA IN THE 20TH CENTURY

The Roman Curia is a unique entity in ecclesiastical history. It has developed over the centuries, being reformed as successive pontiffs saw fit. The structure it has today is largely the work of reforms by Pius X, Paul VI, and John Paul II.

To quote the famous Jesuit author and editor Thomas J.Reese: "The organisation and procedures of the Roman Curia are not static; they are evolving today just as they have continually changed throughout the Church's history, responding to different popes and to different historical situations."

The chart opposite should help readers understand the type of organisation that the popes of the 20th century had to work with.

THE ORGANISATION OF THE ROMAN CURIA

THE POPE

- COLLEGE OF CARDINALS
- SYNOD OF BISHOPS

SECRETARIAT OF STATE

- SOSTITUTO
- VICARIATE OF ROME

SACRED CONGREGATIONS
- Doctrine of the Faith
- Oriental Churches
- Divine Worship & Discipline of the Sacraments
- Causes of saints
- Bishops
- Clergy
- Evangelization of Peoples
- Institutes of Consecrated Life and Societies of Apostolic Life
- Catholic Education

TRIBUNALS
- Apostolic Penitentiary
- Roman Rota
- Apostolic Signature

PONTIFICAL COUNCILS
- Laity
- Promoting Christian Unity
- Family
- Justice and Peace
- *Cor Unum*
- Pastoral Care of Migrants and Travelers
- Pastoral Assistance to Health Care Workers
- Interpretation of Legislative Texts
- Interreligious Dialogue
- Social Communications

OFFICES
- Apostolic Camera
- Patrimony of the Holy See
- Prefecture of Economic Affairs
- Prefecture of Papal Household
- Liturgical Celebrations of the Supreme Pontiff

AGENCIES
- Biblical Commission
- Theological Commission
- Committee for International Eucharistic Congresses
- Commission of Sacred Archaeology
- Pontifical Commission for Science and History
- Cardinalitial Commission for Sanctuaries of Pompeii, Loreto and Bari
- Disciplinary Commission
- Secret Vatican Archives
- Archives of Second
- Vatican Council
- Vatican Library
- Fabric of St. Peters
- Institute of Religious Works
- Office of Papal Charities
- Office of Church Statistics
- Publishing House
- Press Office
- L'Osservatore Romano

THE POPES BEGIN TO TRAVEL
THE VATICAN RAILWAY STATION

The entrance to the Vatican City Railway Station, built in 1929. The arms of Pope Pius XI decorate the entrance

The twentieth century saw the popes' beginning once again to travel outside the Vatican, and in 1929 when Mussolini recognised the Vatican City as a fully sovereign state, it became necessary, due to the hundreds of parcels and thousands of letters sent daily to the Vatican, for the city to have its own railway station. And thus was built the magnificent Vatican railway station with its marble waiting chamber, majestic buildings surrounding it and the magnificent Vatican Gardens in which it is set, Pius XI called it the "most beautiful train station in the world."

However if you arrive in Rome by train these days you will probably arrive at Roma Termini, or for the Vatican Roma San Pietro, because the Vatican station is not usually open to the public any more.

Of course this was not always the case and although history shows us that Pius XI never actually left the Vatican, his successors used the station to visit places all over Italy. In the days before air travel and when the very notion of the pope travelling by train, was almost unbelievable, the idea was met by so much enthusiasm by the Italian people that whenever the pope travelled by train he had to make a stop at every station on the way so great was the excitement of the people, with thousands begging for a papal blessing.

The station itself with its two platforms is situated between St. Martha's Sq, and the civil administration block within Vatican City. It links to the Italian rail network which goes from Rome to Viterbo, over a viaduct to the Roma San Pietro station.

Today the Vatican does not use its train station very often, the heliport next to it, the roads, the Italian rail network, and the airports all being used in preference. But especially for the early popes of the 20th century this novel and luxurious mode of transport was certainly a joy and a blessing.

Pope John XXIII arriving at Assisi

Pope John XXIII acknowledges the crowds from the papal train en route to Loreto and Assisi

This photo shows Pope John XXIII's nine-car train being pulled by a steam locomotive passing over the viaduct as it leaves the Vatican State on October 4, 1962 for Loreto and Assisi

POPE LEO XIII

PONTIFICATE FEBRUARY 20, 1878 TO JULY 20, 1903

POPE LEO XIII (FEBRUARY 20, 1878 TO JULY 20, 1903), WAS THE POPE WHO'S REIGN SPANNED TWO CENTURIES. HIS PAPACY SAW ENORMOUS CHANGES IN EUROPEAN SOCIETY, AS SOCIALISM BECAME A DOMINANT POLITICAL FORCE, REFLECTING A GROWTH IN DISILLUSIONMENT AMONG THE WORKING CLASS, WITH WHOM LEO TRIED TO BUILD BRIDGES AND STEM THE FLOW OF ANTI-CLERICAL RHETORIC THAT WAS RESULTING FROM THEIR INCREASING POVERTY.

Leo XIII was the first Pope to be born in the 19th century and the first to die in the 20th century: he lived to the age of 93, the longest living pope. The dawn of the 20th century saw, an increasingly frail Queen Victoria on the throne of Great Britain, Hawaii become official US territory, the birth of the British Labour Party and Count Vincenzo Gioacchino Raffaele Luigi Pecci, 256th reigning pope, better known as Leo XIII, celebrate the 25th year of his pontificate.

Pope Leo XIII, the latest pope in a direct line of succession from St. Peter was the ideal person to usher in the start of a new century for the world's largest Christian Church, a Church representing over half of all Christians and one-sixth of the world's population. A Church that through apostolic succession was, and indeed still is, the continuation of the Christian community founded by Jesus Christ Himself.

"Patient, conciliatory, and wise in the choosing of opportune solutions to problems and then abiding by them, the pontiff displayed a strong will and calm energy in all his actions throughout his pontificate."

By 1900 Leo XIII was already known for his intellectualism, the development of social teaching and his attempts to define the position of the church to modern thinking. Born on March 2 1810, in Carpineto Romano near Rome, he was the sixth of the seven sons of Col. Ludovico Pecci and Anna Prosperi Buzzi. The family, though indisputably noble were by no means wealthy. His initial education was at the Jesuit College in Viterbo. Afterwards studying at the Roman College. In 1832 he was admitted to the Accademia dei Nobili ecclesiastici, he pursued studies in civil and Canon Law at the university of La Sapienza, being ordained in 1837 and appointed a domestic prelate to Pope Gregory XVI. Gregory remarked on his courage during the cholera epidemic of 1837 and appointed him apostolic delegate to Benevento in the States of the Church. There, Mgr. Pecci proved energetic in controlling banditry and also the intrigues of the liberals. Transferred to the same function in Perugia (1841), where he faced similar problems and had a similarly successful outcome and this time by his capable administration, the building of new roads and the establishment of a savings bank for the farmers he won the lasting affection of the populance.

Consecrated titular Archbishop of Damietta, he went to Belgium as nuncio in January 1843. The three years he spent in Belgium were to be of considerable importance in developing his later outlook as pope, representing as they did his sole contact with industrial Europe. Leaving Brussels in 1846 Pecci went to Perugia where he remained as Archbishop until 1878. At the first Vatican Council he >10

POPE LEO XIII
PONTIFICATE FEBRUARY 20, 1878–JULY 20, 1903

MAIN ENCYCLICALS OF THE 87 ISSUED

Aeterni Patris (August 4, 1879)
Renewal of philosophical church thought based on Thomism

Annum Sacrum (May 25, 1899)
Consecration of the human race to the Sacred Heart

Arcanum Divinae (February 10, 1880)
On the concept of family?

Auspicato Concessum (September 17, 1882)
Renewing the Franciscan Third Order

Grande Munus (September 30, 1880)
On SS. Cyril and Methodius

Graves de Communi Re (January 18, 1901)
On Christian Democracy

Providentissimus Deus (November 18, 1893)
On the study of Holy Scripture

Quamquam Pluries (August 15, 1889)
On devotion to St. Joseph

Quod Apostolici Muneris (December 28, 1878)
On Socialism?

Rerum Novarum (May 15, 1891)
On Capital and Labour

An allegorical painting in the Lateran Palace with a very ultramontane bent! It shows Pope Leo XIII seated on Bernini's rendition of the Throne of St. Peter in the Vatican basilica.

Seated as St Peter's Successor, he himself may be an allegory of the Church or even of Christ in His Church.

On his right are what is taken to be personifications of architecture, the arts and poetry who render him (i.e., the Church) tribute. On his left are the personifications of Faith (or theology) clutching the Cross, and philosophy (or reason) holding some books.

In the forefront and turned away is what is believed to be a personification of paganism or error.

Above right: Details of the clasp of an alb belonging to Leo XIII at the Benedictine Abbey at Vallombrosa

voted with the majority but was not an outstanding member. A cardinal from 1853 he became Camerelengo in the Roman Curia in 1877 whilst at the same time retaining his see. At the conclave following Pius IX's death, he was papabile as candidate of the moderates. After receiving 19 votes on the first ballot, compared with six given to the next most favoured choice, Cardinal Bilio, he emerged as pope after the third ballot, with 44 of the 61 votes.

Taking the name Leo XIII, his pontificate was foreseen as being a short one, it in fact lasted for over 25 years and came to be regarded as one of the most significant in modern times, as a result of Leo's numerous teachings, acts of initiative, and exceptional prestige. Patient, conciliatory, and wise in the choosing of opportune solutions to problems and then abiding by them, the pontiff displayed a strong will and calm energy in all his actions throughout his pontificate.

As soon as he was elected to the papacy, Leo XIII worked to encourage understanding between the Church and the modern world. When he firmly re-asserted the scholastic doctrine that science and religion co-exist, he required the study of Thomas Aquinas and opened the Vatican Secret Archives to qualified researchers.

Leo XIII was the first Pope to come out strongly in favour of the French Republic, upsetting many French monarchists. In his relations with the Italian state, Leo XIII continued the Papacy's self-imposed incarceration in the Vatican stance, and continued to insist that Italian Catholics should not vote in Italian elections or hold elected office. Leo XIII was also the first Pope of whom a sound recording was made as well as the first to be filmed with a motion picture camera.

Throughout his time as pope Leo had tried to reconcile the Church with the working class, particularly by dealing with the social changes that were sweeping Europe. The new economic order had resulted in the growth of an impoverished working class, with increasing anti-clerical and socialist sympathies and Leo helped to greatly reverse this trend. By the time of his death on July 20, 1903 Leo had succeeded in bringing normalcy back to the Church after the tumultuous years of Pius IX and Leo's intellectual and diplomatic skills, symbolised by that white ascetic silhouette, had helped regain much of the prestige lost with the fall of the Papal States. Commentaries from the entire world at the time of his death gave proof of this.

Despite set backs, Leo XIII's pontificate planted seeds that were eventually to grow into an abundant harvest.

POPE ST. PIUS X

PONTIFICATE AUGUST 4, 1903 TO AUGUST 20, 1914

A FIERCE CRITIC OF MODERNISM AND SUPPPORTER OF THOMAS AQUINAS, **POPE ST. PIUS X** (AUGUST 4, 1903 TO AUGUST 20, 1914) REINVIGORATED THE FAITH IN THE FACE OF INCREASING INDIFFERENCE TO THE TEACHINGS OF THE CHURCH.

At the conclave of 1903 (July 31 to August 4) Giuseppe Melchiorre Sarto was elected as successor to Leo XIII, against his appeals to the contrary. He took the name of Pius, the tenth of that name. He was, in many ways the ideal man to continue with the work started by his predecessor Leo XIII, who had actively promoted a link between the Catholic Church and secular culture; faith and science; and divine revelation and reason. From the very start Pius X defended the Catholic faith against popular 19th century views such as indifferentism and relativism, which his predecessors had equally warned against. He also followed his predecessors example by promoting Thomas Aquinas and Thomism as the only theology to be taught in Catholic institutions. Pius opposed modernism, a theological school of thought, which claimed that Catholic dogma itself should be modernised and blended with 19th century philosophies, viewing that modernism was an import of secular errors.

Giuseppe Sarto was born on June 2, 1835 at Treviso in Italy. His father was the

village postman but it was from his mother, Margarita Sanson, that he received a profoundly Christian influence, which led him after successful studies in the college at Castelfranco, to the seminary at Padua in 1850. His exceptional mind soon became evident, along with "the eminent distinction of his spirit." After his ordination on September 18, 1858 he spent nine years as curate in

Tombolo and eight as priest in Salzano. His success in both of these parishes was such that the bishop of Treviso named him spiritual director of his major seminary and chancellor of the diocese in November 1875.

He was eventually made bishop of Mantua in 1884, where he revitalised the diocese by both his energy and numerous contacts with priests and laity. Transferred to Venice as patriarch and cardinal in 1893 he was noted there for his spirit of poverty, apostolic zeal, concern for divine worship, directives in the field of Catholic action, as well as for his professional, social and political interests. A look at his pastoral letters of this period afford the reader a glimpse of his future work as pope. It was here that his first attacks against what became to be referred to as "modernism" were made. For example his first pastoral to the Venetians solemnly affirmed that, in matters concerning the Vicar of Christ, "there should be no question, no subtleties, no opposing of personal rights to his rights, but only obedience."

Pontificate

At the conclave of 1903, according to historians, the favourite to succeed Leo was the late Pope's secretary of state, Cardinal Mariano Rampolla del Tindaro. On the first ballot, Cardinal Rampolla received 24 votes, Cardinal Gotti had 17 votes, and Cardinal Sarto five votes. On the second ballot Rampolla had gained five votes, as did Sarto. The next day, it seemed that Rampolla would be elected. However, the veto (*ius exclusivae*) against Rampolla's nomination, by Polish Cardinal Jan Puzyna from Cracow in the name of Emperor Franz Joseph (1848-1916) >14

POPE ST. PIUS X
PONTIFICATE AUGUST 4, 1903 TO AUGUST 20, 1914

MAIN ENCYCLICALS OF THE 16 ISSUED

E Supremi Apostolatus (October 4, 1903)
Set out the guiding principles of his pontificate

Pieni L'animo (July 28, 1906)
Pius X's attitude to Modernism

Il fermo proposito (June 11, 1905)
On Catholic Action in Italy

of Austria-Hungary, was proclaimed. Many among the conclave, including Rampolla, protested the veto, and it was even suggested that he be elected pope despite the veto.

However, the third vote had already begun, and thus the conclave had to continue with the voting, which resulted in no clear winner, though it did indicate that many of the conclave wished to turn their support to Sarto, who had 21 votes upon counting. The fourth vote showed Rampolla with 30 votes and Sarto with 24. It seemed clear that the cardinals were moving toward Cardinal Sarto.

On the following morning, the fifth vote of the conclave was taken, and the count had Rampolla with ten votes, Gotti with two votes, and Sarto with 50 votes. Thus, on August 4, 1903, Cardinal Sarto was elected to the 257th pontificate. This marked the last time a veto would be exercised by a Catholic monarch in the proceedings of the conclave.

At first, it is reported, Sarto declined the nomination, feeling unworthy. Additionally, he had been deeply saddened by the use of the Austro-Hungarian veto and vowed to rescind these powers and excommunicate anyone who leaked information during a conclave. With the cardinals asking him to reconsider, it is further reported, he went into solitude, and took the position after deep prayer and the urging of his fellow cardinals. Pius X's traditional coronation took place on the following Sunday, August 9, 1903.

Once elected Vicar of Christ he started as he meant to go on. His first encyclicle, *E supreme Apostolatus* on October 4, 1903 together with his speech to the sacred College on November 9 formulated the guiding pricipled of the rest of his pontificate, namely to battle against estrangement from God and against apostasy. In his own words he sought "to restore all things in Christ, in order that Christ might be all and in all." In no area of human activity, he promised, would he fail to affirm the authority of God, the rigorous obedience due His church, and the limitless extent of the papal mission. His naturally extended to politics and foreign affairs so far as they concerned the faith and on his election he immediately appointed Cardinal Merry del Val, secretary of the conclave, his secretary of state. In a direct continuation of Leo XIII's pontificate he, from the very start, sought to promote both social justice and charity, which he saw as the sole guarantee of real order and peace among individuals and groups.

It was, however, against what he termed "Modernism" that Pius fought his fiercest battle. Modernism and relativism, in terms of their presence in the Church, were theological trends that tried to assimilate modern philosophers like Kant into church theology arguing that beliefs of the Church have evolved throughout its history and continue to evolve. Anti-modernists viewed these notions as contrary to the dogmas and traditions

> **"Pius opposed modernism, a theological school of thought, which claimed that Catholic dogma itself should be modernised and blended with 19th century philosophies, viewing that modernism was an import of secular errors."**

of the Catholic Church. In a decree, entitled *Lamentabili sane exitu* (or "A Lamentable Departure Indeed"), issued July 3, 1907 Pius X formally condemned 65 modernist or relativist propositions concerning the nature of the Church, revelation, biblical exegesis, the sacraments, and the divinity of Christ. This was followed by the encyclical *Pascendi Dominici Gregis* (or "Feeding the Lord's Flock"), which characterised Modernism as the "synthesis of all heresies." Following these, Pius X ordered that all clerics take the *Sacrorum antistitum*, an oath against Modernism. He also encouraged the formation and efforts of *Sodalitium Pianum* (or League of Pius V), an anti-Modernist network of informants.

Pius X's aggressive stance against modernism caused some disruption within the Church. Although only about forty clerics refused to take the oath, Catholic scholarship with modernistic tendencies was substantially discouraged. Theologians who wished to pursue lines of inquiry in line with secularism, modernism, or relativism had to stop, or face conflict with the papacy, and possibly even excommunication.

Pius X's grief at the outbreak of the First World War, appeared in his exhortation Dum Europa Fer of August 2, 1914 already weakened from a heart attack in 1913, the declaration of war, reportedly sent the 79 year old pope into a state of melancholy and horror, he died on August 20, 1914.

The cardinals of the Roman Curia requested on February 24, 1923 the introduction of his cause and after long investigation from 1923 to 1946, the approval of the required miracles and the ritual formalities, Pius X was beatified on June 3, 1951 and canonised on May 29, 1954. ■

POPE BENEDICT XV

PONTIFICATE SEPTEMBER 3, 1914 TO JANUARY 22, 1922

THE HORROR OF THE FIRST WORLD WAR CAST A LONG SHADOW OVER THE PAPACY OF **POPE BENEDICT XV** (SEPTEMBER 3, 1914 TO JANUARY 22, 1922), AND HIS FAILURE TO BRING ABOUT A PEACEFUL SETTLEMENT TO THE CONFLICT LEFT HIM BITTERLY DISAPPOINTED.

Giacomo Paolo Giovanni Battista Della Chiesa was born into the patrician classes of Genoa on November 21, 1854. To his parents, Marchese Giuseppe Della Chiesa and Giovanna Migliorati he was a constant cause for concern, as a result of a birth injury, one eye one ear and one shoulder were noticeably higher than the other, he was short and extremely thin, with a pronounced limp throughout his life, this delicate health and small stature however, which effectively prevented him playing with other children, did though promote his early acquired studious habits and his tendency to solitude and introspection. His elementary education came from private tutors, his secondary from diocesan priests at the Instituto Donavaro e Giusso. From an early age Giacomo wanted to study for the priesthood but his father fearing the anti clericalism of the time, asked him to defer his priestly ambition and instead to attend the Royal University of Genoa, where he received a doctorate in civil law. It was only after this that his father acquiesced to his son's persistent request to study for the priesthood, at the seminary his small stature earned him the nickname "piccoletto," – "tiny."

Finally ordained in 1878 he received a doctorate in theology in 1879 and one in Canon Law in 1880, his potential was soon spotted by Archbishop Rampolla who invited he young priest to join >18

MAIN ENCYCLICALS OF THE 12 ISSUED

Ad beatissimi Apostolorum (November 1, 1914)
The inaugural encyclical, a blueprint for what he hoped of his pontificate

Humani Generis Redemptionem (June 15, 1917)
On preaching the word of God

Pacem Dei munus (May 23, 1920)
A plea for the restoration of brotherly love after the First World War

Spiritus Paraclitus (September 15, 1920)
A plea for the return to the study of Holy Writ

Tomb of Benedict XV in St. Peter's Basilica

POPE BENEDICT XV
PONTIFICATE SEPTEMBER 3, 1914 TO JANUARY 22, 1922

the staff of the Papal Secretariat of State and Rampolla became apostolic nuncio to Spain in 1882 he took Della Chiesa with him as his secretary. Not longer after their arrival in Spain a violent cholera epidemic broke out and the two organised relief for the victims and even acted as male nurses for a while, this experience was to stand the future Benedict XV in good stead during the first world war when he soon grasped the need to organise Vatican relief work for victims of the war.

In 1887 Rampolla was named as papal secretary of state and raised to the rank of cardinal, the young Chiesa moved with him as his secretary, finally becoming undersecretary of state in 1901. Della Chiesa's gracious and aristocratic style of diplomacy was in contrast to the somewhat choleric approach of Cardinal Rampolla and the two complimented each other well. When Merry Del Val replaced Rampolla as secretary of state and Pius X succeeded Leo XIII, Della Chiesa was initially retained in his post as under secretary but as a protégé of Rampolla the new pope distrusted him and when in 1907 the position of nuncio to Spain became vacant it was presumed that the role would be his, however Pius instead appointed him Archbishop of Bologna but at the same time witholding until 1914 the traditional cardinals hat that went automatically with the job, therefore becoming a cardinal just three months before the conclave that elected him pope. The conclave of 1914 was brief and the need for a pope with diplomatic skills to handle a world at war was tantamount. Della Chiessa was not regarded at its opening as one of the leading papabili, but he was elected on the tenth ballot on September 3. The coronation took place on September 6, on a very modest scale due to the war.

Immediately after the election the new Benedict XV made sweeping changes in the personnel of the Roman Curia, Merry Del Val was immediately removed from the office of secretary of state, (without it is said, the time to even sort his papers). Right from the start of Benedict's pontificate it was to be the war that overshadowed everything. The sheer

horror of the war with its carnage, death and destruction horrified the sensitive pope, who directed all his efforts towards attempting a diplomatic solution and in relief work for the victims of the conflict. However his refusal to take sides under any circumstances only led to both sides accusing him of favouring the other. In 1917 he proposed a seven point peace plan, which he sent to the heads of the central and allied powers. The main thrust of the plan was to be the waiving of war damage compensation claims by both sides, the Germans readily agreed, but as the vast majority of the damage had actually been perpetrated by them during their invasion of Belgium and France, the Allies viewed the plan as favouring Germany. Add to this the German offer of assistance to the pope in recovering Rome, in the wake of the defeat of Italy and it wasn't long before even the clergy in France began to refer to the "Boche Pope." This continuing confrontation with Italy over the Vatican's attempts to recover Rome, "The Roman Question" further paralysed his efforts at peace although his exertions at this time, resulting in secret meetings with Cardinal Gasparri and Benito Mussolini, did pave the way to the eventual Lateran Pacts of 1929.

The debacle of his peace efforts were perhaps the greatest disappointment that Benedict XV suffered in his entire pontificate, and after its collapse he did not raise his voice again until after the end of the war, with his encyclical Pacem Dei munus (May 23, 1920) in which he pleaded for the restoration of brotherly love. In the long run Benedict's main efforts to improve the effects of the war were in the vast amounts of money he spent to aid the wounded, refugees and displaced people, 82,000,000 Lira in total, leaving the Vatican treasury empty.

In 1922, to the surprise of all, after a short illness lasting only a few days, Pope Benedict XV died. This pope, renowned for his generosity, not only of spirit but of material goods, had so depleted the Vatican coffers with his constant alms giving that the Holy See found itself having to borrow money to bury him.

It was widely said that throughout his life Giacomo Della Chiesa was incapable of sustaining rancour or of harbouring grudges, his aim, as stated in many of the 12 encyclicals he wrote, was to accomplish peace between nations, among social classes and within the Church itself.

POPE PIUS XI

PONTIFICATE FEBRUARY 6, 1922 TO FEBRUARY 10, 1939

THE ASTONISHING RISE FROM THE HUMBLE POSITION OF VATICAN LIBRARIAN TO THE PAPACY OF **POPE PIUS XI** (FEBRUARY 6, 1922 TO FEBRUARY 10, 1939), HIGHLIGHTS AN ASTONISHING INTELLECT AND THIRST FOR WIDENING THE CHURCH'S APPEAL.

Before being elected pope, Achille Ratti, who took the name Pius XI, had spent virtually the whole of his working life as a librarian, firstly at the Ambrosiano in his native Milan and secondly at the Vatican itself.

This distinguished scholar of medieval manuscripts and keen mountaineer was born Ambrogio Damiano Achille Ratti in Desio, Milan on May 31, 1857, the son of an owner of a silk factory. After ordination in 1879 and studies at the Gregorian University, Rome he became a professor at the major seminary in Milan and was appointed to the staff of the Ambrosian Library, Milan, where he remained from 1888 to 1911. From 1911 to 1918 Ratti worked at the Vatican Library, first as pro-prefect and after 1914 as prefect. It was then, in 1919 that Ratti's strange rise to the top began, he was suddenly, and many thought mysteriously, taken from the Vatican Library, consecrate titular Archbishop of Lepanto and sent as nuncio to Poland, then just emerging from Tsarist rule, and where the Catholic Church was under major reconstruction.

In the consistory of June 3, 1921, Pope Benedict created three new cardinals, among them Achille Ratti, who he appointed as Archbishop of Milan simultaneously.

His episcopate in Milan, however, was cut short when, on January 22, 1922, it was announced that Pope Benedict XV had died suddenly that day of pneumonia. At the ensuing conclave (the longest of the 20th century), Ratti was elected Pope on February 6, 1922 on the 14th ballot, taking the name of Pius XI. His first act was to revive the traditional public blessing given from the balcony, *Urbi et Orbi*, ("to the city and to the world"). >22

"After ordination in 1879 and studies at the Gregorian University, Rome he became a professor at the major seminary in Milan and was appointed to the staff of the Ambrosian Library, Milan."

POPE PIUS XI
PONTIFICATE FEBRUARY 6, 1922 TO FEBRUARY 10, 1939

MAIN ENCYCLICALS OF THE 30 ISSUED

Urbi Arcano (Dec 23, 1922)
Inaugurates "Catholic Action" or the "participation of the layman in the hierarchical apostolate"

Quas primas (Dec 11, 1925)
Institutes the Feast of Christ the King

Divini illius magistri (Dec 31, 1929)
Lays the foundations for a Christian educational theory

Casti Connubbii (Dec 30, 1930)
On Christian marriage

Quadragesimo anno (May 15, 1931)
Pius' great social encyclical

Non Abbiamo Bisogno (July 5, 1931)
Against Italian Fascism

Mit brennender Sorge (March 14, 1937)
Against National Socialism

Divini Redemptoris (March 19, 1937)
Against Communism

Pope Pius XI in the Cathedra of St. John Lateran

MI È SOMMAMENTE GRATO INAVGVRARE LA NVOVA RETE TELEFONICA AVTOMATICA DELLO STATO DELLA CITTÀ DEL VATICANO, CHE RAPPRESENTA L' VLTIMO PERFEZIONAMENTO DELLA TELEFONIA ED OFFRIRÀ A QVESTA SANTA CITTÀ VN SERVIZIO DEGNO DELLA SEDE DEL VICARIO DI CRISTO.

19 NOVEMBRE 1930

Pius PP. XI

This is an image of Pope Pius XI's message for the inauguration of the Vatican's first central telephone exchange November 19, 1930. After the Vatican and Italy signed the Lateran Pacts in 1929, the telephones within Vatican City were allowed to be linked up to Rome's and Italy's telephone networks. The Vatican's first telephone exchange was provided by the church in the United States

Pius XI's first encyclical as Pope was directly related to his aim of Christianising all aspects of increasingly secular societies. *Ubi arcano*, promulgated in December 1922, inaugurated the "Catholic Action" movement. The idea was to involve lay men and women in an organisation, under the close supervision of the bishops, which would actively spread Catholic values and political ideas throughout society. Pius XI also gave his approval to specialised movements like the Jocists, associations of young Catholic industrial workers who aimed to Christianise the workforce, and provide a Catholic alternative to Communist and socialist trade unions. Similar goals were in evidence in his encyclicals *Divini illus magistri* (1929), making clear the need for Christian over secular education, and *Casti Connubii* (1930), praising Christian marriage and family life as the basis for any good society, condemning artificial means of contraception, but also acknowledging at the same time the unitive aspect of intercourse as licit.

However it was Pius' ability to mend the long breach between the papacy and the Italian government and to gain recognition once more of the sovereign independence of the Holy See that led to one of his signature achievements, the signing in 1929 of the *Lateran Treaty* with the Italian government and the establishment of an independent Vatican City State.

To bolster his own new regime, Mussolini was also eager for an

Pope Pius XI is seen kneeling amid the brilliant assembly in St. Peter's during the veneration of the relics of Blessed Don Bosco after his beatification. The entire Diplomatic Corps attached to the Holy See and a great gathering of prelates were among the vast congregation

agreement. After years of negotiation, in 1929, the Pope supervised the signing of the Lateran Treaties with the Italian government. According to the terms of the first treaty, Vatican City was given sovereignty as an enclave of the city of Rome in return for the Vatican relinquishing its claim to the former territories of the Papal States. Pius XI thus became a head of state (albeit the smallest state in the world), the first Pope who could be termed as such since the Papal States fell after the unification of Italy in the 19th century A second treaty, the concordat with Italy recognised Roman Catholicism as the official state religion of Italy, gave the Church power over marriage law in Italy (ensuring the illegality of divorce), and restored Catholic religious teaching in all schools. In return, the clergy would not take part in politics. A third treaty provided financial compensation to the Vatican for the loss of the Papal States.

After the success of the treaties however the Vatican's relationship with Mussolini gradually deteriorated as the nature of his totalitarian government became more and more obvious and as a consequence Pius issued the encyclical *Non Abbiamo Bisogno* in 1931, in which he criticised the idea of a totalitarian state and Mussolini's treatment of the Church.

Pius XI was eager to negotiate concordats with any country that was willing to do so, thinking that written treaties were the best way to protect the Church's rights against governments increasingly inclined to interfere in such matters. Twelve concordats were signed during his reign with various types of governments. Adolf Hitler became Chancellor of Germany on January 30, >24

Pope Pius XI in St. Paul's Basilica, Rome. The Holy Father went to St. Paul's to offer Mass for the ex-Servicemen's Peace Pilgrimage to Rome, and there addressed the war veterans

POPE PIUS XI
PONTIFICATE FEBRUARY 6, 1922 TO FEBRUARY 10, 1939

Pope Pius XI, listens to the address of Guglielmo Marconi, the inventor of radio, during a 1933 ceremony inaugurating the world's first station for radio communication by ultrashort wave. The radio-telephone system invented by Marconi linked the Vatican with the pope's summer residence in Castel Gandolfo. Seated by the pope is Cardinal Granito Pignatelli di Belmonte, then dean of the College of Cardinals

1933 and asked for a concordat, Pius XI accepted. Negotiations were conducted on his behalf by Cardinal Eugenio Pacelli, later Pope Pius XII. The Reichskonkordat was signed by Pacelli and by the German government in June 1933, and included guarantees of liberty for the Church, independence for Catholic organisations and youth groups, and religious teaching in schools. The ink however was hardly dry on the document when the Nazi's began systematically ignoring all it contained.

In the closing year of his pontificate Pius reached a standing that was little short of phrophetic and firmly placed him in the position of one of the outstanding characters of the twentieth century, a man of simple, sober character, Pius was always adverse to any form of ostentation. Quite conscious of the fragile nature of world peace at that time, he made every effort to strengthen the will to peace and to contain racialism and excessive nationalism which he saw as being the major threat to that peace. Pius died shortly before the outbreak of the war and was interred in the grotto under St. Peter's. ■

The first papal phone, donated to Pope Pius XI by Catholics in the United States, was used by popes for decades until the end of Pope John XXIII's pontificate. After that the phone in the pope's apartments was a standard phone in papal white

Cardinal Pacelli (the future Pius XII) pictured here with Pope Pius XI who appointed him Cardinal-Priest of Santi Giovanni e Paolo on December 16, 1929 and within a few months, on February 7, 1930 also appointed him Cardinal Secretary of State. In 1935, he named the Cardinal Camerlengo of the Holy Roman Church

POPE PIUS XI
PONTIFICATE FEBRUARY 6, 1922 TO FEBRUARY 10, 1939

THE LATERAN AGREEMENT

BEFORE THE UNIFICATION OF ITALY IN 1861, THE POPE WAS THE RULER (IN A CIVIL AS WELL AS A SPIRITUAL SENSE) OF A NUMBER OF TERRITORIES ON THE ITALIAN PENINSULAR. THESE TERRITORIES KNOWN AS THE PAPAL STATES WERE FORMED IN THE SIXTH CENTURY AND OVER THE COMING CENTURIES, AS THE POPE BECAME ITALY'S MOST POWERFUL SECULAR RULER, AS WELL AS HEAD OF THE CHURCH, THEIR SIZE AND AUTHORITY INCREASED ACCORDINGLY.

However when the French Revolution broke out it proved as disastrous for the temporal territories of the Papacy as for the Catholic Church in general. The Papal States were invaded, a Roman republic declared and the Pope himself fled to France, dying in exile there in 1799. With the fall of the Napoleonic System in 1814 the Papal States were restored and until the death of Pope Gregory XVI in 1846 the Popes ruled their temporal states with full Kingly authority.

The 1840s found Italy (largely under Habsburg, Austrian domination) divided and fractious and when in 1848/49 nationalist and liberal revolutions broke out across the whole of the continent, Italy followed suit with another Roman Republic being declared and once again the pope fleeing the city. Though soon restored by French and Austrian troops, the Pope and the Papal States were quickly in trouble again this time caught in the cross fire of Italian nationalism, with both sides, republicans and monarchists alike seeing the Papal States as the chief obstacle to Italian unity.

Benito Mussolini reads his credentials prior to signing the Lateran Treaty on behalf of King Victor Emmanuel III. Cardinal Gasparri (seated), signed on behalf of Pope Pius XI

After the Second Italian War of Independence, much of northern Italy was unified under the House of Savoy but after Garibaldi's overthrow of the Bourbons in the Kingdom of the two Sicilies, the Sardinians, fearing a southern republican government and capitalising on the general dissatisfaction with the Papal States, conquered two thirds of them, in 1860, Bologna, Ferrara, Umbria, the Marches, Benevento and Pontecorvo were all formally annexed and by November of that year a unified Kingdom of Italy declared.

> **"Immediately after his election on February 6, 1922, Pius XI indicating his eagerness to terminate the long embittered situation appeared on the front balcony of St. Peter's Basilica to impart his blessing, a gesture unknown since 1870."**

Rome was declared the capital of Italy in March 1861 but the new government was unable to actually take possession of the city as Napoleon III stationed a French garrison in the city in order to protect Pope Pius IX. The collapse of the Second French Empire however forced Napoleon to remove the troops in order to defend France itself. Faced with growing demands for the seizure of Rome King Victor Emmanuel II sent Count Ponza di San Martino to Pius IX with a personal offer, offering a face saving proposal that would have allowed the Italian army into Rome under the guise of protecting the Holy Father. Pius IX's reaction to San Martino was far from friendly and in an ill tempered outburst declared that Victor Emmanuel would never enter Rome. On September 10th Italy declared war on what remained of the Papal States, eventually laying siege to Rome. Although the Pope's tiny army was incapable of defending the city Pius ordered that they should put up at least token resistance, in order to show the world that the Italians were taking Rome by force and not by consent. On September 20 1870 the city fell and the following October Rome and Latium were annexed to the Kingdom of Italy.

A bitter and furious Pius confidently expected the Catholic World to rally to his aid but it did not. The Italian government guaranteed to the Pope and his successors the use of the Vatican and the Lateran Palaces and a yearly income of 3,250,000 lire as indemnity for the loss of sovereignty and territory but Pius refused, claiming the necessity for independence of any political power. The former papal palace, the Quirinal, had also become the royal palace of the King of Italy and Pius withdrew into the Vatican itself, where he lived as a self proclaimed "prisoner" refusing to leave or to set foot in St. Peter's Sq. and even going so far as to forbid Catholics on pain of excommunication to participate in elections in the new Italian state.

For the next 59 years this state of affairs, that became known as "The Roman Question," poisoned all dealings between the Vatican and the Kingdom of Italy. However immediately after his election on February 6, 1922, Pius XI indicating his eagerness to terminate the long embittered situation appeared on the front balcony of St. Peter's Basilica to impart his blessing, a gesture unknown since 1870. The Italian Prime Minister Benito Mussolini had already shown a desire for reconciliation and negotiations for a settlement finally began in 1926, culminating in the Lateran Pacts of 1929. Signed for King Victor Emmanuel III by Mussolini and for Pope Pius XI by Pietro Cardinal Gasparri, Papal Secretary of State. The agreements included a political treaty, which created the state of Vatican City and guaranteed to the Holy See full and independent sovereignty. The Pope was pledged to perpetual neutrality in international affairs and to abstention from mediation except when specifically requested by all parties to a controversy. Also agreed on were a concordat establishing Roman Catholicism as the religion of Italy and a financial arrangement awarding money to the Holy See in settlement of all its claims against Italy, arising from the loss of temporal power in 1870. In 1947 the Lateran Agreements were incorporated into the constitution of the new Italian republic and in 1984 an agreement was signed, revising the concordat, which among other things ended the Church's position as the state supported religion of Italy. ■

> **"The Pope was pledged to perpetual neutrality in international affairs and to abstention from mediation except when specifically requested by all parties to a controversy."**

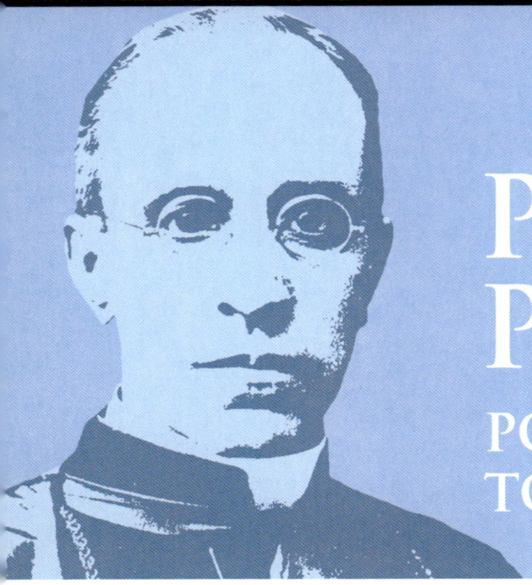

POPE VENERABLE PIUS XII

PONTIFICATE MARCH 2, 1939 TO OCTOBER 9, 1958

HISTORY IS NOW STARTING TO RE-EVALUATE THE RECORD OF **POPE PIUS XII** (MARCH 2, 1939 TO OCTOBER 9, 1958), THE MAN WHO GUIDED THE CHURCH THROUGH THE FEAR AND AND HORROR OF WORLD WAR II.

Cardinal Pacelli, secretary of state, knelt beside the narrow bed on which lay the body of Pope Pius XI, and intoned the "De Profundis," Achille Ratti had been his friend as well as his pope and it was with great emotion that he kissed his brow, called out "Achille, Achille, twice, as tradition demanded, straightened and announced, "the Pope is dead!"

It was February 10,1939, and the tall, ascetic figure of Cardinal Eugenio Pacelli was already one of the best-known figures in the Church. Seemingly born to be pope, it was on March 2, 1939, his 63rd birthday, that Cardinal Eugenio Maria Giuseppe Giovanni Pacelli became pope. As he took off his cardinals' robe and was dressed in the papal cassock of pure white, he repeated again and again the words "miserere mei" – Have pity on me.

Eugenio's grandfather, Marcantonio Pacelli, was under-secretary in the papal ministry and founded the Vatican's newspaper, *L'Osservatore Romano* in 1861; his father, Filippo Pacelli, a Franciscan tertiary, was the dean of the Sacra Rota Romana.

In this September 1945 image of, Pope Pius XII, wearing the ring of St. Peter, raises his right hand in papal blessing as he sits upon his throne in the Vatican

On May 13, 1917 Pacelli was created titular archbishop of Sardes by Benedict XV and at the same time appointed nuncio to Bavaria. He eventually became nuncio to Germany in 1920. >30

Pope Pius XII is carried by attendants during a December 24, 1950, ceremony at the Vatican. In the same year, the pontiff declared as dogma the belief in the Assumption of the Blessed Virgin

POPE VENERABLE PIUS XII
PONTIFICATE MARCH 2, 1939 TO OCTOBER 9, 1958

MAIN ENCYCLICALS OF THE 41 ISSUED

Mystici Corporis Christi (June 29, 1943)
On the Mystical Body of Christ and the Church

Communium Interpretes (April 15, 1945)
On Ending the Second World War

Deiparae Virginis Mariae (May 1, 1946)
Should We Define the Assumption?

Humani Generis (August 12, 1950)
Concerning Some False Opinions Threatening to Undermine the Foundations of Catholic Doctrine

Ingruentium Malorum (September 15, 1951)
On Reciting the Rosary

Fulgens Corona (September 8, 1953)
Proclaiming a Marian Year to Commemorate the Centenary of the Definition of the Dogma of the Immaculate Conception

Ad Caeli Reginam (October 11, 1954)
On Proclaiming the Queenship of Mary

Musicae Sacrae (December 25, 1955)
On Sacred Music

Haurietis Aquas (May 15, 1956)
On Devotion to the Sacred Heart

The pope rushes to be with his people immediately after the Allied air-raid on Rome, as captured in this impressive picture of August 13, 1943

His first months as pope were spent in doing all he could to avert the looming threat of world war right until the last moment, declaring on August 24, "nothing is lost by peace; everything is lost by war." Once the war started he vowed to take no side in the struggle but to promote peace at every opportunity, to seek to prevent atrocities and inhumanity and to alleviate suffering wherever possible. This stance became daily more difficult and by the time the Nazi genocide against the Jews was beginning to be known, the leader of Catholic Christendom was finding it impossible to keep the Holy See "above the strife of parties."

The whole of Pius' ethos had always sought the diplomatic solution, believing papal condemnations would only exacerbate the Nazi persecution and make things, if possible, even worse for the Jews of Europe. But by 1942 the pressure on him to speak out was so great that he decided to give a clear and unequivecol condemnation of the Nazi genocide. So in his Christmas address of that year he concluded, it was the duty of all mankind to help bring society back under the rule of God, it was a duty he declared that was owed by all to the war dead, to their mothers, their widows and their orphans, to those exiled by war, and to "the hundreds of thousands of innocent people put to death or doomed to slow extinction, sometimes merely because of their race or their descent."

Mussolini and the Germans were furious but not all felt that the condemnation

Pope Pius XII is welcomed to Castel Gandolpho by the town's mayor, Marcello Costa (who at the time, aged 27 was the youngest mayor in Italy). This picture, dated August 1954, from from the archives of *The Universe*, goes on to inform readers that the Holy Father's Cadillac was preceded on the journey by one containing his nephew, Prince Carlo Pacelli, and also the pope's lifelong friend, Count Enrico Galeazzi, who was the director of the Vatican's technical and economic services

Cardinal Eugenio Pacelli, is seen during a visit to Budapest, Hungary, on June 11 1938, Pope Benedict XVI has authorised the Vatican Secret Archives to make available to researchers all the documentation from the pre-World War II pontificate of Pope Pius XI. During this pontificate, Cardinal Pacelli served as a nuncio to Germany and then as Vatican secretary of state

Pope Pius XII leaves Castel Gandolfo to return to the Vatican in a Cadillac on November 27, 1943

"His first months as pope were spent in doing all he could to avert the looming threat of world war right until the last moment, declaring on August 24, "nothing is lost by peace; everything is lost by war." Once the war started he vowed to take no side in the struggle but to promote peace at every opportunity, to seek to prevent atrocities and inhumanity and to alleviate suffering wherever possible."

was enough and the allies demanded something more.

The charge that he somehow refused to help the Jews because of anti Semitism is a charge that only later and after his death became fashionable.

In the meantime Vatican funds were poured into rescue measures for the Jews, Pius himself contributed his total private funds to them. After the German occupation of Rome in September 1943 Pius responded to Jewish pleas to supply them with 15 kilos of gold as part of the 50 demanded of them by the Nazis as a ransom for the safety of the Roman Jews. Cloister regulations in religious houses were lifted in order to supply refuge to over 5,000 Jews apart from the large number in the Vatican itself. After the war the Chief Rabbi of Rome converted to Catholicism and took the baptismal name of Eugenio.

Much of Pius' pontificate has now been overshadowed by the war but during his 19 years as he published 41 encyclicals as well as composing a huge number of other documents.

He defended the Church against ideological attacks, every bit as damaging as war and bombs, and he was undoubtedly the person most responsible for preparing the Church for the Second Vatican Council. Pope Pius XII was a holy man who spoke out fearlessly when necessary and inspired in many others his own all-abiding love for God.

POPE VENERABLE PIUS XII
PONTIFICATE MARCH 2, 1939 TO OCTOBER 9, 1958

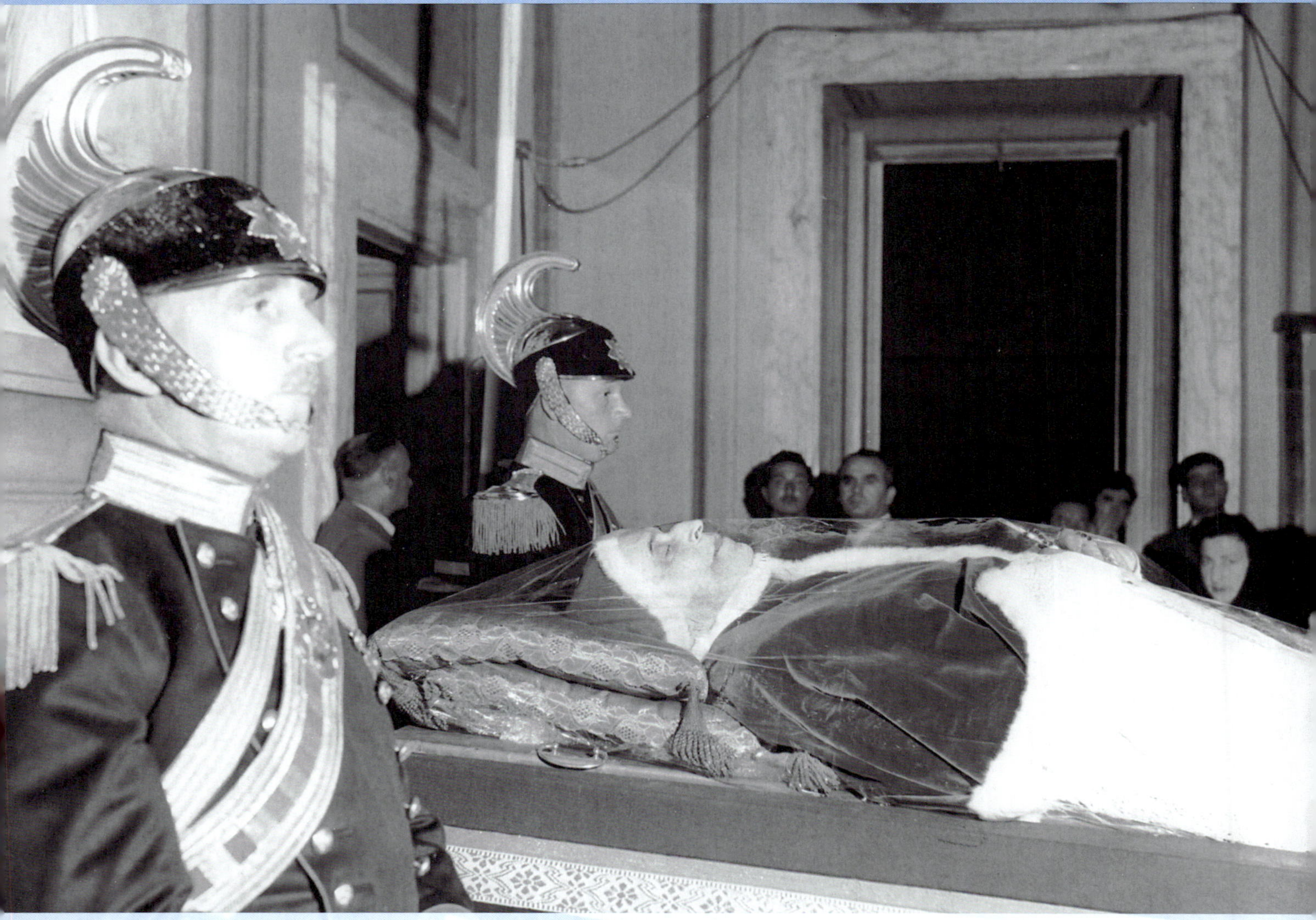

The body of Pope Pius XII lies in state at the papal summer residence, Castel Gandolfo, outside Rome on October 9, 1958. A noble guard of the Papal Court stands at his head

THE POPE'S DOCTOR
BY ALAN MCELWAIN

One day in 1929, a tall, frail-looking prelate from the Vatican walked into a Rome oculist's rooms to be fitted with a new pair of spectacles.

From that moment there began a strange friendship between the churchman and the doctor that was to last for the next 29 years.

The prelate was Eugenio Pacelli, destined to become Pope Pius XII. The oculist, who was also a surgeon, was Riccardo Galeazzi-Lisi. He was with the Pope when he died, at Castelgandolfo, on October 9, 1958. Then he was banished from the Vatican for infamous conduct.

After he became Pope in 1939, Pius XII appointed Galeazzi-Lisi his personal physician. For the rest of the Pope's life, the doctor was one of his cherished

A general scene at the foot of the altar in the Basilica of St. Peter in Vatican City on October 13, 1958 during the funeral service for Pope Pius XII

confidants. He made Galeazzi-Lisi an honorary member of the renowned Pontifical Academy of Sciences. He became one of the Vatican's best-known figures, coming and going at will, taken into confidence by many members of the Papal retinue – and, inevitably, envied and resented by others.

This was the man who, owing so much to Pius XII in the Pope's lifetime, rewarded him, in death, by profaning him.

Taking advantage of his professional position, Galeazzi-Lisi stayed interminably at the dying Pope's bedside and, in violation of the rules both of the Vatican and of good taste, took a series of revoltingly candid photographs of the Pope in his death-throes. They were to complement a detailed hour-by-hour diary he kept, setting out, in grisly detail, the Pope's last hours on earth.

Galeazzi-Lisi proceeded to sell story and pictures to publications in Italy and abroad willing to pay top prices for his ghoulish "scoops." In Italy, his articles, liberally illustrated by pictures of the dying Pius XII (and of himself), were on news stands a few hours after the Pope's death. Galeazzi-Lisi had lost no time flogging his wares.

After a storm of protest in Italy and elsewhere, Galeazzi-Lisi had no option but to resign his post as head of the Vatican medical services. The College of Cardinals, conducting the Church's business pending the election of a new Pope, promptly and without comment, accepted the resignation. The speed with which they got rid of Galeazzi-Lisi reflected their distress and indignation over his behaviour.

They had even more against him. The Pope's body would normally have been embalmed in readiness for the traditional lying-in-state in St. Peter's but Galeazzi-Lisi contrived, in some inexplicable way, to keep it from the regular embalmers. He virtually took the body into his own keeping. With brash self-confidence, he and an associate had worked out an embalming system of their own. This, they claimed, although based on ancient formulas, was superior to modern methods and would ensure that Pope Pius' body would resist contamination for at least 100 years. And, of course, if the system, following its spectacular debut, turned out to be a lucrative proposition on the funeral-markets, they wouldn't be averse from that.

The Galeazzi-Lisi miracle system involved encasing the Pope's body in a cellophane bag into which were inserted aromatic herbs, or spices, or some such, used, said one report, by the early Christians, and said another, by the ancient Egyptians, to preserve their dead. It was all mumbo-jumbo. The whole thing was a ghastly failure from the start; all that Galeazzi-Lisi and his accomplice succeeded in doing was profane the Papal corpse. >34

POPE VENERABLE PIUS XII
PONTIFICATE MARCH 2, 1939 TO OCTOBER 9, 1958

A view of the of the final official Requiem Mass for the late Pope Pius XII in St. Peter's Basilica in Vatican City on October 19, 1958. Note the Papal tiara on top of the coffin

When Pope Pius's body, stretched out in its bizarre transparent sheath, was laid on a great raised catafalque in St. Peter's, the multitudes who filed by were horrified to see it literally decomposing before them. When I saw it, several times, it was taking on a progressively yellowish tinge. Each evening, after St. Peter's was closed, Galeazzi-Lisi would climb a ladder to the body and feverishly pour more of his ingredients into the sheath. It was all futile. The funeral of Pope Pius XII came just in time.

More retribution was to follow the Cardinals' expulsion of Galeazzi-Lisi. The Italian Medical Council struck him from its rolls for "infamous conduct." However, the High Court of the Italian Central Health Commission then reversed the council's order on the sheerest technicality; it held that the council had not properly set out its reasons for ousting the doctor. Questions were also asked about him in the Italian Parliament.

Galeazzi-Lisi blustered and protested his innocence for weeks after the storm broke. He argued cold-bloodedly that professional secrecy "died with the patient." Audaciously, he requested a press conference at the Foreign Press Association. He arrived with his "embalming" colleague and, having argued that there was nothing objectionable about the photographs he had taken, paradoxically produced a nauseating set of them to prove it.

Nothing more was heard of him for a couple of years. Then, in the only interview he had given since the scandal, he spoke in his own defence. He had been traveling about a bit before I heard he was installed in a flat not far from his old Vatican stamping ground. I couldn't imagine him agreeing to revive the objectionable business, but I phoned him up on the off-chance. He invited me to see him.

He had an elegant apartment in a new block. He was a shy, mild-mannered, bespectacled little man. He said: "I have been the victim of Vatican intrigue and envy in professional quarters. I have suffered for far too long as a scapegoat for others." He said he intended to take the odd step of appealing to the Court of Cassation, Italy's highest legal tribunal, against the decision in his own favour of the High Court of the Italian Central Health Commission. This meant the council could not bar him from practicing in Italy until it had reopened the case and given him the opportunity of appearing before it again to speak in his own defence.

"I have built up a huge file and now have all the evidence I need to clear myself," he said. "But, believe me, this time I will not keep silent. My past silence stemmed from a warning Pope Pius gave me never to get involved in press controversies. This has been interpreted as admission of guilt on my part and my enemies have got away with things for which I have been carrying the blame."

Unrepentant to the end, he asked me to make a special point of his denial that he ever took any of the much-condemned photographs of Pope Pius's last hours. Other people had plenty of opportunity for taking the prohibited pictures, he insisted, because the Pope died not in the Vatican but at his summer residence in Castelgandolfo, 15 miles from Rome. I couldn't follow this reasoning but let it go. He did admit, superfluously, that he wrote the article about Pope Pius, but, he said, it appeared ten days after other doctors called in for consultation had given press interviews, and there was not much difference between what he wrote and what had already been said.

And, he added, a year before his death. Pope Pius had authorised him to keep a diary about himself and also to take exclusive pictures. Many of these appeared in Galeazzi-Lisi's book, "In the Shadow and Light of Pius XII," published by the top French publishing house, Flammarion.

When I saw him, he said he had closed an extensive Rome practice, but was performing operations in special cases and practising as a consultant. He had patients in various parts of Europe, he claimed, and in Canada, which he had visited not long before, and he was about to go to London to attend some cancer sufferers.

But he stayed mostly in retirement, spending six months of each year in San Remo, on the Italian Riviera. The public heard nothing of him until, in 1968, his family announced his death – after he had been quietly buried with only a few members of the family and close friends present. He was 77.

He left a queer reminder of himself in his palmier days which always intrigued me when I happened to glance up at a building on the corner of Via del Tritone and Via Sistina, in the heart of Rome. Galeazzi-Lisi had had rooms on the first floor of the building. Ethical restrictions on professional advertising being sparse in Italy, he had had his name emblazoned in metal letters about two feet high on two sides of the premises. These had been taken down when he vacated the rooms, but they had been there for so long that a faint impression of the name, Galeazzi-Lisi, could still be seen. ■

This article first appeared in "Annals Australia."

POPE VENERABLE PIUS XII
PONTIFICATE MARCH 2, 1939 TO OCTOBER 9, 1958

"I WILL NOT LEAVE ROME AND MY DUTY EVEN IF IT MEANS I SHOULD DIE"

ON THURSDAY MORNING, OCTOBER 9, 2008, THE HOLY FATHER, **POPE BENEDICT XVI**, PRESIDED AT A PONTIFICAL MASS IN ST. PETER'S BASILICA TO COMMEMORATE THE 50TH ANNIVERSARY OF THE DEATH OF **PIUS XII**. AFTER THE CELEBRATION THE POPE WENT TO THE VATICAN GROTTOS TO PRAY AT THE FORMER PONTIFF'S TOMB. THE FOLLOWING IS A TRANSLATION OF THE HOLY FATHER'S HOMILY, DELIVERED IN ITALIAN.

"Your Eminences,
Venerable Brothers in the Episcopate and in the Priesthood.

Dear Brothers and Sisters,
The passage from the Book of Sirach and the Prologue to St. Peter's First Letter, proclaimed as the First and Second Readings, offer us important ideas for reflection at this Eucharistic celebration during which we are commemorating my Venerable Predecessor, the Servant of God Pius XII.

Exactly 50 years have passed since his death in the early hours of 9 October 1958. Sirach, as we have heard, reminded whomever intended to follow the Lord that they must prepare themselves to face trials, difficulties and suffering.

He recommended that in order not to succumb to them they needed an upright and steadfast heart, patience and fidelity to God as well as firm determination in pursuing the path of good.

Suffering refines the heart of the Lord's disciple, just as gold is purified in the crucible: "Accept whatever is brought upon you," the sacred author writes, "and in changes that humble you be patient. For gold is tested in the fire,

Pope Benedict XVI in St. Peter's Basilica at the Vatican during the October 9, Mass commemorating the 50th anniversary of Pope Pius XII's death. Pope Benedict defended Pope Pius, saying he worked "secretly and silently" during World War II to "avoid the worst and save the greatest possible number of Jews"

and acceptable men in the furnace of humiliation" (2:4-5).

In the passage that has been presented to us, St. Peter, for his part, goes further when he asked Christians of the communities of Asia Minor, which were being "afflicted by various trials," to "rejoice" in spite of all (1 Pt 1:6).

Trial is in fact necessary, he observes, "so that the genuineness of your faith, more precious than gold which though perishable is tested by fire, may redound to [your] praise and glory and honour at the revelation of Jesus Christ" (I Pt 1:7).

And then for the second time he urges them to rejoice, indeed to exult, with "unutterable and exalted joy" (v. 8). The profound reason for this spiritual rejoicing is to be found in love for Jesus and the certainty of his invisible presence. It is he who makes the faith and hope of believers indestructible, even in the most arduous and complicated events of life.

In the light of these biblical texts we may interpret the earthly life of Pope Pacelli and his long service to the Church, which began in 1901, under Leo and continued with St. Pius X, Benedict XV and Pius.

Above all, these biblical texts help us to understand from what source he drew courage and patience in his Pontifical ministry during the tormented years of the Second World War and in the post-war period, equally complex, of reconstruction and of the difficult international relations which have passed into history known by the significant appellative "Cold War."

"Miserere mei, Deus, secundum magnam misericordiam tuam:" with this invocation of Psalm 51[50], Pius XII began his Testament. And he continued: "These words, which, aware of my unworthiness and insufficiency, I pronounced at the moment in which with trepidation I accepted the election as Supreme Pontiff, I now repeat with even greater justification." At the time he had two years to live.

Abandonment in the merciful hands of God: this was the attitude constantly cultivated by my Venerable Predecessor, the last of the Popes to have been born in >38

POPE VENERABLE PIUS XII
PONTIFICATE MARCH 2, 1939 TO OCTOBER 9, 1958

Pope Benedict XVI descends to the grotto of St. Peter's Basilica at the Vatican October 9 to view the crypt of Pope Pius XII on the 50th anniversary of his death

Rome, who belonged to a family which had been close to the Holy See for years.

In Germany, where he had been Apostolic Nuncio, first in Munich and then in Berlin until 1929, he was appreciated especially for having collaborated with Benedict XV in the attempt to stop the "senseless slaughter" of the Great War and for having realised from the outset, the danger constituted by the monstrous National-Socialist ideology with its pernicious anti-Semitic and anti-Catholic roots.

He was created a Cardinal in December 1929 and, shortly afterwards, became Secretary of State. For nine years he was a faithful collaborator of Pius XI, in an epoch marked by various brands of totalitarianism: Fascist, Nazi and Soviet-Communist, which he respectively condemned in the Encyclicals Non abbiamo bisogno, Mit brennender sorge and Divini Redemptoris.

"He who hears my word and believes... has eternal life (Jn 5:24). Jesus' assurance, which we heard in the Gospel, reminds us of the hardest years of Pius XII's Pontificate when, realising the lack of any human security, he also felt the strong need to cleave to Christ – the one certainty that never fails – through a constant, ascetic effort.

The light of God's Word

The Word of God thus became a light on his journey, a journey on which Pope Pacelli had to console evacuees and the persecuted; he had to wipe away tears of pain and mourn the innumerable victims of the War. Christ alone is man's true hope; only by trusting in him can the human heart open itself to the love that conquers hate.

This knowledge accompanied Pius XII in his ministry as Successor of Peter, a ministry that began precisely when the menacing clouds of a new world war were gathering over Europe and the rest of the world. He sought to avoid this conflict in every way. "The danger is

imminent, but there is still time. Nothing is lost with peace; all can be lost with war!," he had cried in his Radio Message of 24 August 1939 (AAS, XXXI, 1939, P. 334).

The war highlighted the love he felt for his "beloved Rome," a love attested by the intense charitable work he promoted on behalf of the persecuted, without distinction of religion, race, nationality or political affiliation.

When the city was occupied and he was repeatedly advised to leave the Vatican to seek safety, his determined answer was always the same: "I will not leave Rome and my duty even if it means I should die" (cf. Summarium, p. 186).

Relatives and other witnesses also mentioned the deprivation of food, heating, clothes, comforts to which he voluntarily subjected himself in order to share the condition of the people, so harshly tried by the bombing and the consequences of war (cf. A. Torniclli, Pius XII, Un uomo sul trono di Pietro).

And how can we forget his Christmas Radio Message in December 1942? His voice broken by emotion, he deplored the situation of "hundreds of thousands of men and women who, without any fault of their own, sometimes only because of their nationality or race, have been consigned to death or to a slow decline" (AAS, XXXV, 1943, p. 23), with a clear reference to the deportation and extermination of the Jews.

He often acted secretly and silently because, in the light of the practical situations of that complex period of history, he foresaw that only in this way could he avoid the worst and save the greatest possible number of Jews.

Numerous and unanimous attestations of gratitude for his interventions were addressed to him at the end of the war, as well as at the time of his death, from the highest authorities of the Jewish world such as, for example, Israel's Minister for Foreign Affairs Golda Meir, who wrote: "When fearful martyrdom came to our people, the voice of the Pope was raised for its victims. The life of our times was enriched by a voice speaking out about great moral truths above the tumult of daily conflict" and concluded with emotion: "We mourn a great Servant of peace."

Unfortunately, the debate in history on the figure of the Servant of God Pius XII – which has not always been the calmest – failed to highlight all the aspects of his multi-faceted Pontificate. He addressed an enormous number of Discourses, Allocutions and Messages to scientists, doctors, exponents of the most widely varied categories of work. Today, some of these are still extraordinarily relevant and continue to be a reliable reference point. Paul who was his faithful >40

“Abandonment in the merciful hands of God: this was the attitude constantly cultivated by my Venerable Predecessor, the last of the Popes to have been born in Rome, who belonged to a family which had been close to the Holy See for years.”

POPE VENERABLE PIUS XII
PONTIFICATE MARCH 2, 1939 TO OCTOBER 9, 1958

collaborator for many years, described him as an erudite man, a scholar, open to modern forms of research and culture, and whose fidelity both to the principles of human rationality and to the intangible deposit of the truth of the faith was always firm and consistent.

Paul VI considered him a precursor to the Second Vatican Council (cf. Angelus, to March 1974). From this perspective many of his documents deserve mention, but I limit myself to citing just a few.

In the Encyclical Mystici Corporis, published on 29 June 1943 while the War was raging, he described the spiritual and visible relations that unite people with the Incarnate Word and suggested integrating in this perspective all the principal themes of ecclesiology, offering for the first time a dogmatic and theological synthesis that was to form the basis of Lumen gentium, the Conciliar Dogmatic Constitution on the Church.

A few months later, on 20 September 1943, with the Encyclical Divino afflante Spiritu, he established the doctrinal norms for the study of Sacred Scripture, bringing to the fore its importance and role in Christian life. This is a Document that witnesses to great openness to scientific research on the biblical texts.

How can we fail to mention this Encyclical while the work of the Synod is underway on precisely "The Word of God in the Life and Mission of the Church?"

It was thanks to the prophetic intuition of Pius XII that a serious study of the characteristics of ancient historiography was initiated, for a better understanding of the nature of the Sacred Books that does not diminish them or deny their historical value.

Textual criticism

The examination of "literary genres" which aimed at understanding better what the sacred author had wished to express was viewed with some suspicion until 1943, partly because of the abuses that had occurred. The Encyclical recognised its correct application, declaring legitimate its use not only for the study of the Old Testament but also of the New.

"In the present day indeed this art which is called textual criticism and which is used with great and praiseworthy results in the editions of profane authors, is also quite rightly employed in the case of the Sacred Books, because of that very reverence which is due to the Word of God," the Pope explained.

And he added: "for its very purpose is to ensure that the sacred text be restored, as perfectly as possible, be purified from the corruptions due to the carelessness of the copyists and be freed, as far as may be done, from glosses and omissions,

from the interchange and repetition of words and from all other kinds of mistakes, which are wont to make their way gradually into writings handed down through many centuries" (Divino afflante Spiritu, n. 17; AAS XXXV, 1943, p. 336).

The third Encyclical I would like to mention is Mediator Dei, on the liturgy, published on 20 November 1947. With this Document, the Servant of God gave an impetus to the liturgical movement, insisting on the "chief element of divine worship," that "must be interior. For we must always live in Christ and give ourselves to Him completely, so that in Him, with Him and through Him the heavenly Father may be duly glorified," he wrote. "The sacred liturgy requires that these two elements be intimately linked with each other... Otherwise religion clearly amounts to mere formalism, without meaning and without content" [n.24].

Then we cannot omit to mention the considerable impetus that this Pontiff gave to the Church's missionary activity with the Encyclicals Evangelii praecones (1951) and Fidei donum (1957): bringing to the fore every community's duty to proclaim the Gospel to the peoples, as the Second Vatican Council was to do with courageous energy. Moreover, Pope Pacelli demonstrated his love for the missions at the very beginning of his

> **"He often acted secretly and silently because, in the light of the practical situations of that complex period of history, he foresaw that only in this way could he avoid the worst and save the greatest possible number of Jews."**

Pontificate, when in October 1939, he chose to ordain personally 12 Bishops from mission countries, among whom were one Indian, one Chinese and one Japanese Prelate, the first African Bishop and the first Bishop of Madagascar.

Finally, one of his constant pastoral concerns was the promotion of the role of lay people, so that the ecclesial community could avail itself of all available energies and resources. For this too, the Church and the world are grateful to him.

Dear brothers and sisters, while we pray that the cause of Beatification of the Servant of God Pius XII may proceed successfully, it is good to remember that holiness was his ideal, an ideal that he, did not fail to propose to all. It was for this reason that he promoted the causes of Beatification and Canonisation of people who belonged to different nations, people from all the states of life, roles and professions and allowed ample room for women. As a sign of steadfast hope, he held up to humanity Mary herself, the Woman of salvation, proclaiming the Dogma of the Assumption during the Holy Year of 1950.

In our world, assailed as it was then by preoccupations and worries about its future, in this world where, perhaps more than in any other epoch, the distancing of many from truth and virtue lets us glimpse scenarios devoid of hope, Pius XII invites us to turn our gaze to Mary, taken up into heavenly glory.

He invites us to call on her confidently, so that she may make us appreciate increasingly the value of life on earth and help us to turn our gaze to the true destination to which we are all bound: eternal life which, as Jesus assures us, those who listen to and obey his words already possess. Amen!

Taken from:
L'Osservatore Romano
Weekly Edition in English
October 15, 2008

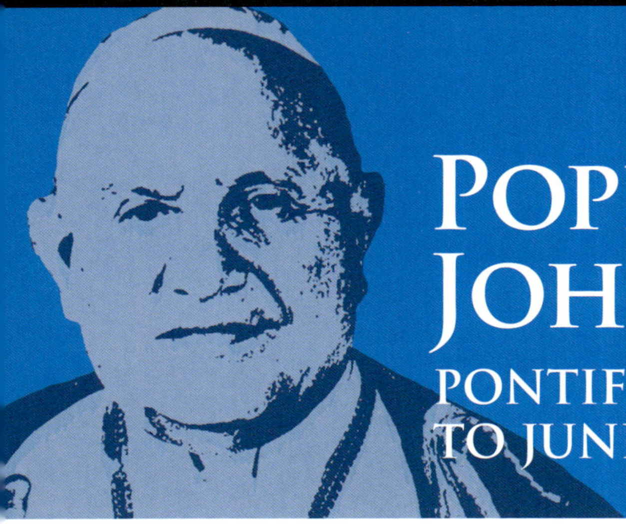

POPE BLESSED JOHN XXIII

PONTIFICATE OCTOBER 28, 1958 TO JUNE 3, 1963

THOUGH POPE FOR JUST FIVE YEARS, **POPE JOHN XXIII** (OCTOBER 28, 1958 TO JUNE 3, 1963) IS FONDLY REMEMBERED AS A MAN WHO RADIATED THE PEACE OF THE LORD TO ALL WHO MET HIM.

Blessed Pope John XXIII was born Angelo Giuseppe Roncalli at Sotto il Monte, Italy, in the Diocese of Bergamo on November 25, 1881. He was the fourth in a family of 14.

He entered the Bergamo seminary in 1892. Here he began the practice of making spiritual notes, which he continued in one form or another until his death, and which have been gathered together in the Journal a Soul. In 1896 he was admitted to the Secular Franciscan Order by the spiritual director of the Bergamo seminary, Fr. Luigi Isacchi; he made a profession of its Rule of life on May 23, 1897.

From 1901 to 1905 he was a student at the Pontifical Roman Seminary. On August 10, 1904 he was ordained a priest. In 1905 he was appointed secretary to the new Bishop of Bergamo, Giacomo Maria Radini Tedeschi.

These were the years of his deepening spiritual encounter with two saints who were outstanding pastors: St. Charles Borromeo and St. Francis de Sales. They were years, too, of deep pastoral involvement and apprenticeship, as he spent every day beside "his" Bishop, Radini Tedeschi. When the Bishop died in 1914, Fr. Angelo continued to teach in the seminary and to minister in various pastoral areas.

When Italy went to war in 1915 he was drafted as a sergeant in the medical corps and became a chaplain to wounded

Then-Cardinal Angelo Giuseppe Roncalli, Pope John XXIII, visits with school children

"Meek and gentle, enterprising and courageous, simple and active, he carried out the Christian duties of the corporal and spiritual works of mercy: visiting the imprisoned and the sick, welcoming those of every nation and faith, bestowing on all his exquisite fatherly care."

soldiers. When the war ended, he opened a student house for the spiritual needs of young people.

In 1919 he was made spiritual director of the seminary, but in 1921 he was called to the service of the Holy See. Benedict XV brought him to Rome to be the Italian president of the Society for the Propagation of the Faith. In 1925 Pius XI named him Apostolic Visitator in Bulgaria, raising him to the episcopate with the titular Diocese of Areopolis. For his Episcopal motto he chose Oboedientia et Pax, which became his guiding motto for the rest of his life.

On March 19, 1925 he was ordained bishop and left for Bulgaria. He was granted the title Apostolic Delegate and remained in Bulgaria until 1935, visiting Catholic communities and establishing relationships of respect and esteem with the other Christian communities. In the aftermath of the 1928 earthquake his solicitude was everywhere present. He endured in silence the misunderstandings and other difficulties of a ministry on the fringes of society, and thus refined his sense of trust and abandonment to Jesus crucified. >44

POPE BLESSED JOHN XXIII
PONTIFICATE OCTOBER 28, 1958 TO JUNE 3, 1963

Pope John XXIII reads his radio and televison address from Castelgandolfo, Italy, to the closing ceremony of the 37th World Eucharistic Congress gathered at Munich, Germany on August 7, 1960. The police estimated that one-and-a-quarter million people came from all parts of the world, not including communist-ruled nations whose authorities denied permission to Roman Catholics to attend. Pope John prayed for true peace in the world "founded on respect for the rights of the church and the dignity of man."

Pope John XXIII, walks with HM The Queen, in the Throne Hall of the Vatican, during an audience on May 5, 1961. The two are followed by The Duke of Edinburgh

In 1935 he was named apostolic delegate in Turkey and Greece.
The Catholic Church was present in many ways in the young Turkish republic. His ministry among the Catholics was intense, and his respectful approach and dialogue with the worlds of Orthodoxy and Islam became a feature of his tenure. When the Second World War broke out he was in Greece. He tried to get news from the prisoners of war to their families and assisted many Jews to escape by issuing "transit visas" from the Apostolic Delegation. In December 1944 Pius XII appointed him Nuncio in France.

During the last months of the war and the beginning of peace he aided prisoners of war and helped to normalise the ecclesiastical organisation of France.
He visited the great shrines of France and participated in popular feasts and in important religious celebrations. >46

POPE BLESSED JOHN XXIII
PONTIFICATE OCTOBER 28, 1958 TO JUNE 3, 1963

MAIN ENCYCLICALS OF THE 8 ISSUED

Ad Petri Cathedram (June 29, 1959)
On Truth, Unity and Peace in a Spirit of Charity

Mater et Magistra (May 15, 1961)
On Christianity and Social Progress

Pacem in Terris (April 11, 1963)
On Establishing Universal peace in truth, justice, charity and liberty

He was an attentive, prudent and positive observer of the new pastoral initiatives of the Bishops and clergy of France. His approach was always characterised by a striving for Gospel simplicity, even amid the most complex diplomatic questions. The sincere piety of his interior life found expression each day in prolonged periods of prayer and meditation. In 1953 he was created a Cardinal and sent to Venice as Patriarch. He was filled with joy at the prospect of ending his days in the direct care of souls, as he had always desired since becoming a priest. He was a wise and enterprising pastor, following the model pastors he had always venerated and walking in the footsteps of St. Laurence Giustiniani, first Patriarch of Venice. As he advanced in years his trust in the Lord grew in the midst of energetic, enterprising and joyful pastoral labours.

At the death of Pius XII he was elected Pope on October 28, 1958, taking the name John XXIII. His pontificate, which lasted less than five years, presented him to the entire world as an authentic image of the Good Shepherd. Meek and gentle, enterprising and courageous, simple and active, he carried out the Christian duties of the corporal and spiritual works of mercy: visiting the imprisoned and the sick, welcoming those of every nation and faith, bestowing on all his exquisite fatherly care. His social magisterium in the Encyclicals Pacem in terris and Mater et Magistra was deeply appreciated.

He convoked the Roman Synod, established the Commission for the Revision of the Code of Canon Law and summoned the Second Vatican Council. He was present as Bishop in his Diocese of Rome through his visitation of the parishes, especially those in the new suburbs. The faithful saw in him a reflection of the goodness of God and called him “the good Pope.” He was sustained by a profound spirit of prayer. He launched an extensive renewal of the Church, while radiating the peace of one who always trusted in the Lord. Pope John XXIII died on the evening of June 3, 1963.

The glass casket of Pope John XXIII is displayed near the main altar inside St. Peter's Basilica June 3, the 38th anniversary of his death. The casket was later moved to its new permanent resting place at the basilica's altar of St. Jerome

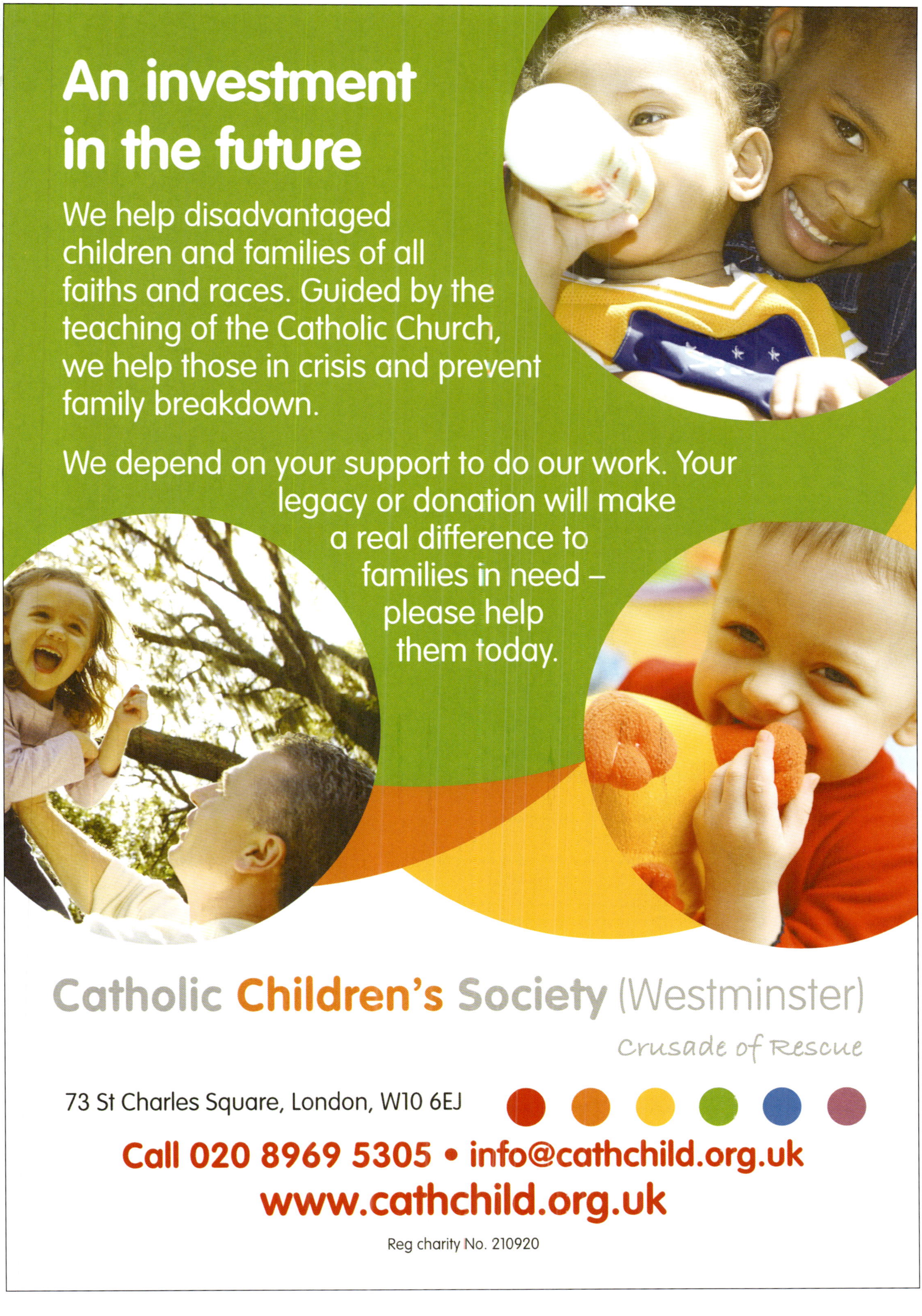
An investment in the future
We help disadvantaged children and families of all faiths and races. Guided by the teaching of the Catholic Church, we help those in crisis and prevent family breakdown.
We depend on your support to do our work. Your legacy or donation will make a real difference to families in need – please help them today.
Catholic Children's Society (Westminster)
Crusade of Rescue
73 St Charles Square, London, W10 6EJ
Call 020 8969 5305 • info@cathchild.org.uk
www.cathchild.org.uk
Reg charity No. 210920

POPE BLESSED JOHN XXIII
PONTIFICATE OCTOBER 28, 1958 TO JUNE 3, 1963

"THOU ART PETER"
THE CORONATION OF A POPE

Although the last pope to be actually crowned was Paul VI, he decided to cease wearing a papal tiara within weeks of his coronation, and laid his own on the altar of St. Peter's Basilica in a gesture of humility. John XXIII however was crowned (with the papal tiara of 1877) and continued to wear it, when the occasion demanded, throughout his pontificate. The papal coronation itself is the ceremony in which a new pope is crowned as earthly head of the Roman Catholic Church, sovereign of Vatican City, and Monarch of the Holy See.

November 4, 1958 saw heavy rain falling on Rome, and hours before the papal procession arrived at the doors of St. Peter's tens of thousands of people were standing in St. Peter's Sq. and down the broad Via della Conciliazione ending at the Tiber.

The new pope coming into St. Peter's could have seen only some hundreds in the piazza, but eventually these numbers grew to 250,000 or more. Tens of thousands were already gathered in the nave of the basilica, and as the time drew nearer, they saw a succession of distinguished persons and delegations being escorted to the tribunes – erected for the burial rites of Pius XII – on either side and beyond the Papal Altar.

Then they saw the Archbishops and Bishops filling the stalls below them – rows and rows of mitred figures. The walls of St. Peter's had been hung with red and gold damask. Over to the right the bronze statue of St. Peter was, for this day, robed in a rich cope and had upon its head a jewelled crown.

A tapestry showing the image of Pope John XXIII hangs from the facade of St. Peter's Basilica September 3. He was beatified along with Pope Pius IX and three other churchmen at a ceremony led by Pope John Paul II

Earlier on spectators described the "sombre light" coming through the high windows, but suddenly, as waves of cheering from outside and the call of the trumpets announced the Pope's coming, thousands of lights were switched >50

The Papal Tiara of Pope Pius VII (1800-1823) which was a gift from Napoleon Bonaparte is shown at an exhibition in Montreal. The tiara contains precious stones looted from the Vatican in 1798 by Napoleon but was too small for the pope's head

POPE BLESSED JOHN XXIII
PONTIFICATE OCTOBER 28, 1958 TO JUNE 3, 1963

on illuminating the whole scene. Floodlights bathed the Papal Altar and sanctuary in a white brilliance to bring the ceremonies to television viewers all over the world. The coronation of Pius XII had in fact been the first to be filmed and the first coronation to be broadcast live on the wireless.

The Sovereign Pontiff, mitred, seated upon the sedia gestatoria, borne by 12 damask-robed men under a canopy was robed in a splendid cope, escorted by the helmeted Noble Guard, and by Swiss Guard shouldering their halberds. At the doors the throne was lowered, and the Cardinal Archpriest and the Canons of St. Peter's went forward one by one to pay their homage.

The procession resumed and, through a sea of cheers and fluttering handkerchiefs, went up the wide way in the centre of the nave, preceded by the bearer of the papal cross, and the clergy carrying, together with the Triple Crown, the mitres – one of them the jewelled Precious Mitre – which the pope would wear during the Mass.

At a point about a third of the way the cheering died away, and the procession, turning right, went to the Chapel of the Blessed Sacrament. The Holy Father descended, his mitre was removed, and with the members of his court he knelt and prayed in silence.

Returning to the nave, the procession went to the chapel of St. Gregory. Here while the pope sat in his throne, the cardinals came to pay him homage. Terce was sung and the pope vested for Mass. His Holiness now appeared like every bishop vested for Pontifical High Mass, but with the striking addition of the fanone, a short cape over his shoulders, consisting of two pieces of silk striped in white, red, and gold, the lower lying under and the other lying over the uppermost vestment, the chasuble. >52

“Receive the Tiara of Three Crowns, and know that you are the Father of Princes and Kings, Guide of the World, Vicar of Our Saviour Jesus Christ, to whom is all honour and glory for ever and ever, amen.”

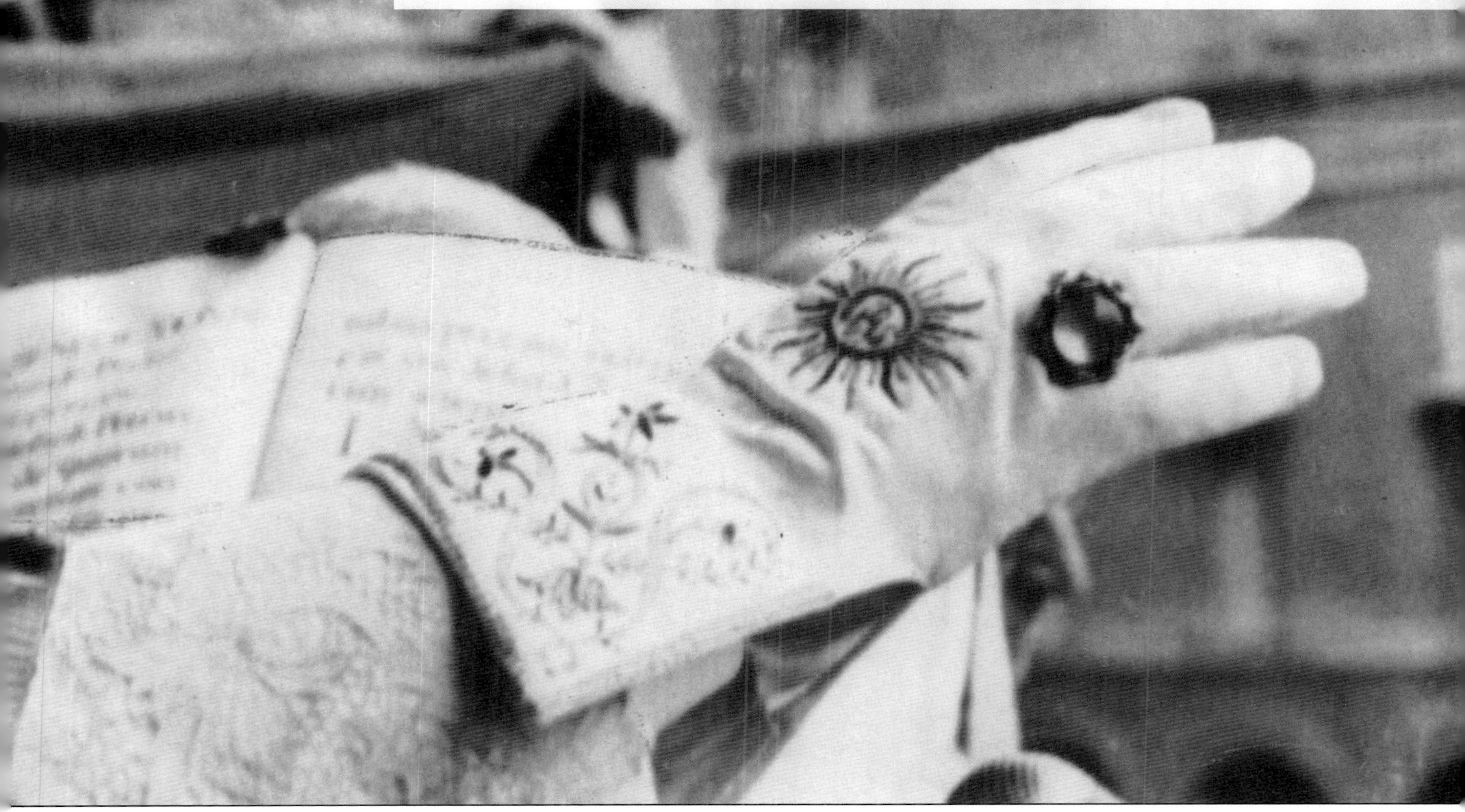

POPE BLESSED JOHN XXIII
PONTIFICATE OCTOBER 28, 1958 TO JUNE 3, 1963

Mounting the sedia again, the pope was borne – while the Sistine Choir sang the "Tue s Petrus" – towards the Altar of the Chair, the Chair of St. Peter. But amidst all this splendour, and as he approached the sanctuary, there came a magnificent reminder. A priest walked before him, carrying a gilt pole with a trumpet – like top, into which he put some flax. Three times he turned, set light to the flax and, as it flared up, cried out in Latin: "Holy Father, so passes the glory of the world."

In the middle of the sanctuary the sedia gestatoria was lowered, and the Holy Father, with the Cardinal deacons, went to the foot of the altar – the altar under the high baldacchino supported by twisted columns – and began the Mass.

Several times His Holiness went from the altar to the brilliantly illuminated canopied throne set up by the Altar of the Chair, that is at the far end of the sanctuary, a long church's length away. Soon after the Mass began, at the *Introit*, the two Cardinal deacons invested him, over his shoulders, with the pallium, the symbol of the fullness of his episcopal power.

Soon too the Cardinal Deacon, accompanied by prelate-judges of the Sacred Roman Rota, and with masters of ceremonies and Consistorial advocates descended the steps beneath the altar leading to the crypt, and there, over the tomb of St.Peter, they invoked the first pope's intercession for the new pope, one of his 20th century successors.

The Consecration and Elevation were especially solemn. The 30,000 people, the Cardinals, Archbishops, Bishops, and priests, were kneeling, heads bowed, as, in a profound silence, the Sovereign Pontiff, bowing over the altar, uttered the words of Transubstantiation. He genuflected and from high up in the dome, from silver trumpets, flowed silveri's serene, beautiful melody. Then, as the pope raised the Sacred Host in his hands, swords and halberds were lowered in salute.

Complete silence returned as His Holiness bowed again over the chalice; and then came the sharp sounds of the salute by Noble Guard and Swiss Guard, and the consoling melody from the dome.

Many people had been in the basilica for five hours when the Mass ended, the Pope, in the midst of repeated cheers, went out of the basilica in procession, turning constantly to each side to bless the people.

Soon the packed multitude in the square saw prelates coming on to the balcony. As the crowds gazed upon the wide and deep tapestry of the papal arms suspended from the ledge, their eyes travelled upwards and there they saw the Sovereign Pontiff, with cardinals and members of his court, coming in procession.

The gathering there was of course comparatively small, and the ceremony brief. Noble Guard stood sentinel at the far ends. The decorated fans of ostrich feathers were on each side of the throne. Some of the cardinals were there, with prelates and lay members of the court, and the custodian of the Triple Crown. The pope still wearing his Mass vestments had at either hand the two Cardinal Deacons.

Prayers were said, mitres were removed, and Mgr. Enrico Dante, the master of ceremonies, coming from the left of the pope, took off his mitre too. Then Cardinal Canali came forward from the pope's right, received the Triple Crown from its cushion and placed it upon the Holy Father's head, addressing him in words expressing his spiritual authority and fatherhood.

"Receive the Tiara of Three Crowns, and know that you are the Father of Princes and Kings, Guide of the World, Vicar of Our Saviour Jesus Christ, to whom is all honour and glory for ever and ever, amen."

The Sovereign Pontiff rose to a storm of cheering in the square below, greeted the people with movements of his hands, and then, with a gentle embracing motion, brought his hands together. He raised his right hand above his head, the applause died down, and turning to the left, to the centre, and to the right, His Holiness gave his threefold blessing.

He remained on the balcony a little to renew his greetings then went away back to the Vatican. Between four and five hours had passed since he left the Vatican to go into St.Peter's. There were no festivities in the Vatican Palace. The Pope, as all popes do, ate alone, and for the rest of the day he was engaged in his prayers and his work. ■

POPE PAUL VI

PONTIFICATE JUNE 21, 1963 TO AUGUST 6, 1978

NO POPE HAS OVERSEEN AS MUCH CHANGE IN THE WAYS OF THE CHURCH AS **POPE PAUL VI** (JUNE 21, 1963 TO AUGUST 6, 1978), THE MAN KNOWN AS THE 'FIRST MODERN POPE.'

Pope Paul VI is often referred to as "the first modern pope" and it was during his reign from 1963-1978 that more changes were introduced in the Catholic Church than in all the previous centuries combined, not least due to the Second Vatican Council.

Giovanni Battista Enrico Antonio Maria Montini was born in Concesio, in the province of Brescia, Lombardy, on September 26, 1897. The second son of a wealthy landowner and editor of the Catholic newspaper, *Il Cittadino di Brescia* as well as a parliamentary deputy.

Having requested admission to the diocesan seminary he was initially allowed to live at home and attend lectures whenever he was physically able. He was ordained on May 29, 1920 and was sent to Rome for graduate work in philosophy and Canon law at the Gregorian University and for literature at the University of Rome. In May 1923 he was sent to Warsaw as an attaché of the nunciature there, but again his health intervened and he was recalled back to Rome in the November. Once back in Rome he continued to work for the secretariat of state and thus began his 31 years of work for the department.

In 1931 the future Pope Pius XII Cardinal Pacelli appointed him to teach history at the papal academy for diplomats.

As war broke out, thousands of letters from all parts of the world arrived at the desk of the pope, most of them asking for understanding, prayer and help. >56

Pope Paul VI greets people gathered outside the papal summer house in Castel Gandolfo, Italy, September 14, 1977. In his encyclical, "Caritas in Veritate" ("Charity in Truth"), Pope Benedict XVI refers often to the 1967 encyclical "Populorum Progressio" ("The Progress of Peoples"), in which Pope Paul focuses on the problem of international development and the gap between the rich and poor

POPE PAUL VI
PONTIFICATE JUNE 21, 1963 TO AUGUST 6, 1978

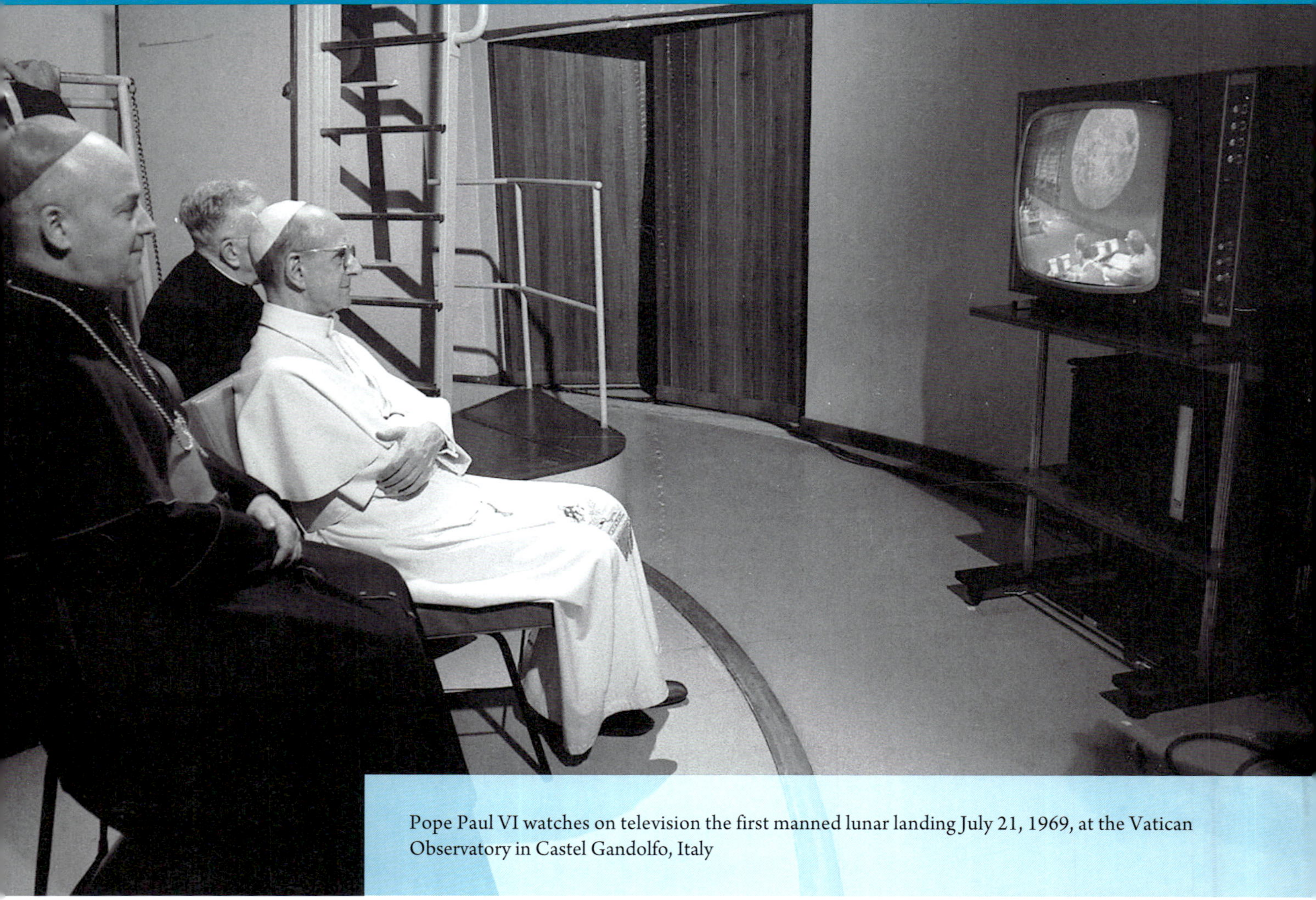

Pope Paul VI watches on television the first manned lunar landing July 21, 1969, at the Vatican Observatory in Castel Gandolfo, Italy

Montini was tasked to reply in the name of Pius XII, expressing his empathy, and understanding and providing help, where possible. At the request of the pope, he created an information office for prisoners of war and refugees.

In 1944, Luigi Maglione died, and Pius XII appointed Tardini and Montini together as heads of the state department.

After the death of Cardinal Schuster in 1954, Montini was appointed Archbishop of Milan, which made him the speaker of the Italian Bishop Conference.

When John XXIII, shortly after his election, elevated 23 prelates to the college of cardinals in 1958, Montini headed the list. During the years preceding Vatican II, Montini was frequently consulted by John XXIII and between the announcement and the convening of the council, Montini delivered three major addresses on the subject and made it the topic of his Lenten pastoral in 1962.

Apollo 11 astronauts Neil Armstrong, Edwin "Buzz" Aldrin and Michael Collins, accompanied by their wives, meet with Pope Paul VI at the Vatican October 16, 1969. The pope called the Apollo 11 mission – the first time man reached the moon – a "sublime victory"

All present knew that Pope John XXIII could not last indefinitely and that a new pope would soon be needed. At the conclave held between June 17-21 following the Pope's death, attended by 80 cardinals, Giovanni Battista Montini >58

Vatican City May 1, 1965. Pope Paul VI is shown delivering from his desk his radio message to the Philippines, for the 400th anniversary of the Catholic Faith in that country. There had been much press speculation that he would be making a papal visit for the occasion, this was not however to be realised until November 1970, five years later

POPE PAUL VI
PONTIFICATE JUNE 21, 1963 TO AUGUST 6, 1978

Pope Paul VI waves the starting flag for the Tour of Italy cycling race from the St. Damasus courtyard at the Vatican in this May 16, 1974 photo

was elected pope. His main project, Vatican II had been a failure, because it did not produce nor end within the one session as anticipated by the late pope.

Paul did away with much of the regal splendour of the papacy. He modified the papal coronation, which his successor would eventually emulate, he donated his own Papal Tiara, to the Basilica of the National Shrine of the Immaculate Conception in Washington, DC (where is it on permanent display in the crypt) as a gift to American Catholics. In 1968, with the motu proprio Pontificalis Domus, he discontinued most of the ceremonial functions of the old Roman nobility at the papal court, save for the Prince Assistants to the Papal Throne. He also abolished the Palatine Guard and the Noble Guard, leaving the Swiss Guard as the sole military order of the Vatican.

Within a few days of his election, Paul VI convoked the second session of the Ecumenical Council for September 29, only three weeks later than the date fixed by his predecessor. Faced with conflicting interpretations and controversies, he redirected the implementation of its reform goals, which included the largest revision to the Church's Liturgy since the Council of Trent (held 400 years prior to Vatican II), until his death in 1978. >60

POPE PAUL VI
PONTIFICATE JUNE 21, 1963 TO AUGUST 6, 1978

MAIN ENCYCLICALS OF THE 7 ISSUED

Ecclesiam Suam (August 6, 1964)
On the Church

Mysterium Fidei (September 3, 1965)
On the Holy Eucharist

Humanae Vitae (July 25, 1968)
On the regulation of birth

During Vatican II, the council avoided statements which might anger Christians of other faiths.

Throughout his pontificate the tension between papal primacy and the collegiality of the episcopacy was a source of conflict. On September 14, 1965 he announced the establishment of the Synod of Bishops called for by the council, but some issues that seemed suitable for discussion by the synod were reserved to himself. Celibacy, removed from the debate of the fourth session of the council, was made the subject of an encyclical, June 24, 1967); the regulation of birth was treated in Humanae vitae July 24, 1968), his last encyclical. The controversies over these two pronouncements tended to overshadow the last years of his pontificate.

Pope Paul had a very poor press and his public image suffered by comparison with his outgoing and jovial predecessor. Those who knew him best, however, describe him as a brilliant man, deeply spiritual, humble, reserved and gentle, a man of "infinite courtesy." He was one of the most travelled popes in history and the first to visit five continents. His remarkable corpus of thought must be searched out in his many addresses and letters as well as in his major pronouncements. His successful conclusion of Vatican II has left its mark on the history of the Church, but history will also record his rigorous reform of the Roman curia, his well-received address to the UN in 1965, his encyclical Populorum

Pope Paul VI and Cardinal Karol Wojtyla meet at the Vatican in this undated photo. Paul VI, who served in Poland during his early priesthood, held the future Pope John Paul II in high regard

> **"Paul did away with much of the regal splendour of the papacy. He modified the papal coronation, which his successor would eventually emulate."**

Bishops fill St. Peter's Basilica as Pope Paul VI presides over a meeting of the Second Vatican Council. Sessions were held in the later months of 1962, 1963, 1964 and 1965. Pope John XXIII opened the council in 1962, stating that the goal of the council was to eradicate seeds of discord and to promote peace and unity among humankind. The remaining three sessions were led by Pope Paul following the death of Pope John in June 1963

progressio (1967), his second great social letter Octogesima adveniens (1971) – the first to show an awareness of many problems that have only recently been brought to light – and his apostolic exhortation Evangelii nuntiandi, his last major pronouncement which also touched on the central question of the just conception of liberation and salvation.

Pope Paul VI, the pilgrim pope, died on August 6, 1978, the feast of the Transfiguration. He asked that his funeral be simple and no monument over his grave. ■

Pope Paul VI makes his way past bishops during a session of the Second Vatican Council in 1964. Paul VI guided the church during its post-Vatican II transition until his death in 1978

Pope Paul VI offers a blessing at Rome's Leonardo da Vinci airport before boarding a flight to Istanbul, Turkey, in 1967. Pope Paul inaugurated the modern papal practice of world travels

Pope Paul VI, right, greets Orthodox Ecumenical Patriarch Athenagoras of Constantinople during the pontiff's 1964 trip to the Holy Land. Pope Paul inaugurated many of the bilateral and multilateral ecumenical dialogues that continue today

POPE JOHN PAUL I

PONTIFICATE AUGUST 26, 1978 TO SEPTEMBER 28, 1978

FOR JUST 33 DAYS, **POPE JOHN PAUL I** (AUGUST 26 TO SEPTEMBER 28, 1978), LED THE CATHOLIC CHURCH... BUT IN THAT SHORT TIME HE MADE A LASTING IMPRESSION ON ALL WHO MET HIM.

Thirty years ago (26th August), a conclave of 111 cardinals elected Italian Cardinal Albino Luciani as Pope John Paul I, the 'smiling Pope' who served only 33 days before dying of a heart attack.

It was one of the briefest pontificates, but it left a lasting impression. Many inside and outside the Vatican felt that a man of extraordinary humility and goodness had passed their way – like a meteor that lights up the sky and quickly disappears, as one cardinal put it.

Albino Luciani was born on October 17, 1912 in Forno di Canale a province of the Veneto region in northern Italy. He was the son of Giovanni Luciani, a bricklayer, and Bortola Tancon.

Luciani entered the minor seminary of Feltre in 1923, where his teachers found him "too lively," and later went on to the major seminary of Belluno. During his stay at Belluno, he attempted to join the Jesuits but was denied by the seminary's rector. Ordained a priest on 7 July 1935, Luciani then served as a curate in his native Forno de Canale before becoming a professor and the vice-rector of the

Belluno seminary in 1937. Among the different subjects, he taught dogmatic and moral theology, canon law, and sacred art.

In 1947, he was named vicar general to Bishop Girolamo Bortignon, OFM Cap, of Belluno. Two years later, in 1949, he was placed in charge of diocesan catechetics. On 15 December 1958, Luciani was appointed Bishop of Vittorio Veneto by Pope John XXIII. He received his episcopal consecration on the following 27 December from Pope John himself. As a bishop, he participated in all the sessions of the Second Vatican Council (1962-1965). On 15 December 1969, he was appointed Patriarch of Venice by Pope Paul VI and took possession of the archdiocese on 3 February 1970. Pope Paul created Luciani Cardinal-Priest of *St. Marco* in the consistory of 5 March 1973.

Only five cardinals who voted in the conclave that elected him pope are still alive. Among them is Cardinal Joseph Ratzinger who at the time was one of the youngest cardinal-electors.

Along with the rest of the College of Cardinals, he watched as Pope John Paul immediately introduced a new style of papacy, more simple and less formal than many at the Vatican were used to.

He explained the concept of free will with a metaphor about prudent car maintenance. He spoke sympathetically about those who can't bring themselves to believe in God. He once jokingly compared marriage to a gilded bird cage: "Those on the outside are dying to get in, while those on the inside are dying to get out."

In one of his most quoted remarks, he said God "is a father, but even more, a mother" in the way he loves humanity. He backed up his statement by quoting the Old Testament prophet Isaiah: "Could a mother forget her child? But even if that were to happen, God will never forget his people."

In 2004, Cardinal Ratzinger travelled to the province of Belluno, the native land of Pope John Paul, and said he was praying for his beatification.

Indeed, even as the possible beatification of Pope John Paul II has attracted much of the Church's attention in recent years, Pope John Paul I's sainthood cause slowly has been working through the system.

The vice postulator of the cause, Mgr. Giorgio Lise, said that the diocesan phase of the documentation has recently been given formal acceptance by the Congregation for Saints' Causes.

Meanwhile, the local approval of a miracle attributed to the intercession of Pope John Paul I – the healing of a malignant lymphoma – is expected to be completed very soon.

The death of Pope John Paul on September 28, 1978, was a shock for the Church and for the cardinals who elected him.

The coffin of Pope John Paul I is carried from St. Peter's Basilica for the funeral Mass on October 4, 1978, at the Vatican

POPE JOHN PAUL II

PONTIFICATE OCTOBER 16, 1978 TO APRIL 2, 2005

FEW PEOPLE HAVE TOUCHED AS MANY LIVES – AND HEARTS – AS **POPE JOHN PAUL II** (OCTOBER 16, 1978 TO APRIL 2, 2005) DID DURING HIS 27 YEARS AS PONTIFF, AND HIS GIFT FOR COMMUNICATING EASILY WITH PEOPLE FROM ALL FAITHS AND NONE TURNED HIM INTO A GLOBAL STATESMAN OF WORLD RENOWN.

Karol Józef Wojtyla, known as John Paul II since his October 1978 election to the papacy, was born in the Polish town of Wadowice, a small city 50 kilometres from Krakow, on May 18, 1920. He was the youngest of three children born to Karol Wojtyla and Emilia Kaczorowska. His mother died in 1929. His eldest brother Edmund, a doctor, died in 1932 and his father, a non-commissioned army officer died in 1941. A sister, Olga, had died before he was born.

Upon graduation from Marcin Wadowita high school in Wadowice, he enrolled in Krakow's Jagiellonian University in 1938 and in a school for drama.

The Nazi occupation forces closed the university in 1939 and young Karol had to work in a quarry (1940-1944) and then in the Solvay chemical factory to earn his living and to avoid being deported to Germany.

In 1942, aware of his call to the priesthood, he began courses in the clandestine seminary of Krakow, run by Cardinal Adam Stefan Sapieha, archbishop of Krakow. At the same time, Karol Wojtyla was one of the pioneers of the "Rhapsodic Theatre," also clandestine.

After the Second World War, he continued his studies in the major seminary of Krakow, once it had re-opened, and in the faculty of theology of the Jagiellonian University. He was ordained to the priesthood by Archbishop Sapieha in Krakow on November 1, 1946. >66

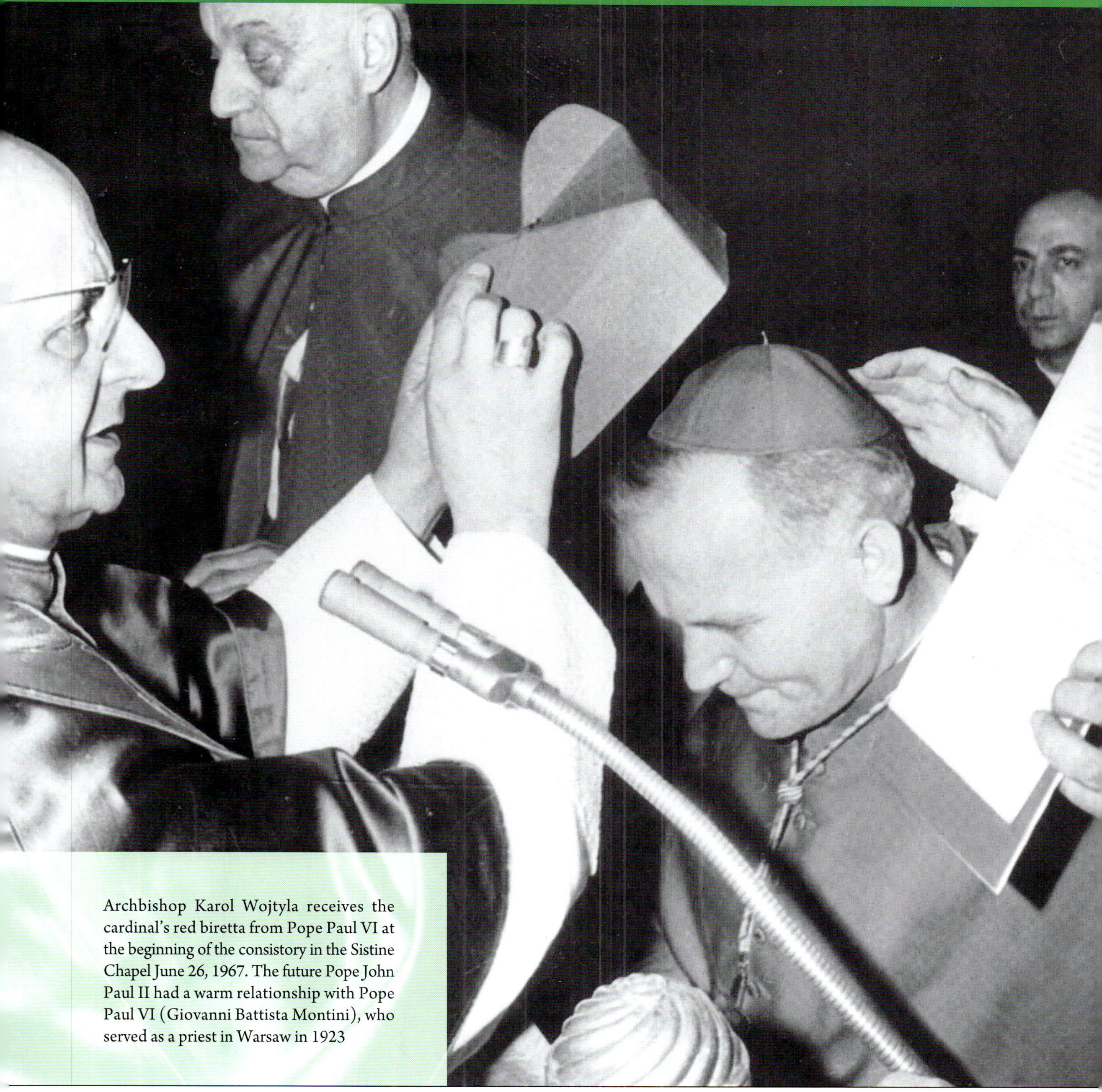

Archbishop Karol Wojtyla receives the cardinal's red biretta from Pope Paul VI at the beginning of the consistory in the Sistine Chapel June 26, 1967. The future Pope John Paul II had a warm relationship with Pope Paul VI (Giovanni Battista Montini), who served as a priest in Warsaw in 1923

POPE JOHN PAUL II
PONTIFICATE OCTOBER 16, 1978 TO APRIL 2, 2005

Pope John Paul II leads the Way of the Cross around Rome's ancient Colosseum on Good Friday, April 21, 2000

Pope John Paul II speaks to students and faculty of Lublin University during a special meeting at the basilica of Jasna Gora monastery in Czestochowa, Poland. The pontiff visited his homeland for the first time as pope in June 1979

Shortly afterwards, Cardinal Sapieha sent him to Rome where he worked under the guidance of the French Dominican, Garrigou-Lagrange. He finished his doctorate in theology in 1948 with a thesis on the subject of faith in the works of St. John of the Cross (Doctrina de fide apud Sanctum Ioannem a Cruce). At that time, during his vacations, he exercised his pastoral ministry among the Polish immigrants of France, Belgium and Holland.

In 1948 he returned to Poland and was vicar of various parishes in Krakow as well as chaplain to university students. This period lasted until 1951 when he again took up his studies in philosophy and theology. In 1953 he defended a thesis on "evaluation of the possibility of founding a Catholic ethic on the ethical system of Max Scheler" at Lublin Catholic University. Later he became professor of moral theology and social ethics in the major seminary of Krakow and in the Faculty of Theology of Lublin.

On July 4, 1958, he was appointed titular bishop of Ombi and auxiliary >68

POPE JOHN PAUL II
PONTIFICATE OCTOBER 16, 1978 TO APRIL 2, 2005

of Krakow by Pope Pius XII, and was consecrated September 28, 1958, in Wawel Cathedral, Krakow, by Archbishop Eugeniusz Baziak.

On January 13, 1964, he was appointed archbishop of Krakow by Pope Paul VI, who made him a cardinal June 26, 1967.

Besides taking part in Vatican Council II (1962-1965) where he made an important contribution, Cardinal Wojtyla participated in all the assemblies of the Synod of Bishops.

> **"His love for young people brought him to establish the World Youth Days. The 19 WYDs celebrated during his pontificate brought together millions of young people from all over the world."**

The Cardinals elected him Pope at the Conclave of October 16, 1978, and he took the name of John Paul II. On October 22, he became pope. His pontificate, one of the longest in the history of the Church, lasted nearly 27 years.

He made 104 pastoral visits outside Italy and 146 within Italy. As bishop of Rome he visited 317 of the city's 333 parishes.

He had more meetings than any of his predecessors with the people of God and the leaders of nations. More than 17,600,000 pilgrims participated in the General Audiences held on Wednesdays (more than 1160), not counting other special audiences and religious ceremonies [more than eight million pilgrims during the Great Jubilee of the Year 2000 alone], and the millions of faithful he met during pastoral visits in Italy and throughout the world. >70

POPE JOHN PAUL II
PONTIFICATE OCTOBER 16, 1978 TO APRIL 2, 2005

MAIN ENCYCLICALS OF THE 11 ISSUED

Redemptor Hominis (March 4, 1979)
The Redeemer of Man

Redemptoris Mater (March 25, 1987)
Mother of the Redeemer

Centesimus Annus (May 1, 1991)
On the 100th anniversary of Pope Leo XIII's Rerum Novarum – On Capital and Labour; On Catholic social teaching

Veritatis Splendor (August 6, 1993)
The Splendor of Truth – Regarding Certain Fundamental Questions of the Church's Moral Teaching

Ecclesia De Eucharistia (April 17, 2003)
On the Eucharist in its Relationship to the Church

We must also remember the numerous government personalities he encountered during 38 official visits, 738 audiences and meetings held with Heads of State, and 246 audiences and meetings with Prime Ministers.

His love for young people brought him to establish the World Youth Days. The 19 WYDs celebrated during his pontificate brought together millions of young people from all over the world. At the same time his care for the family was expressed in the World Meetings of Families, which he initiated in 1994.

John Paul II successfully encouraged dialogue with the Jews and with the representatives of other religions, whom he several times invited to prayer meetings for peace, especially in Assisi.

Under his guidance the Church prepared herself for the third millennium and celebrated the Great Jubilee of the year 2000 in accordance with the instructions given in the Apostolic Letter Tertio Millennio adveniente. The Church then faced the new epoch, receiving his instructions in the Apostolic Letter Novo Millennio ineunte, in which he indicated to the faithful their future path.

With the Year of the Redemption, the Marian Year and the Year of the Eucharist, he promoted the spiritual renewal of the Church. He gave an extraordinary impetus to canonisations and Beatifications, focusing on countless examples of holiness as an incentive for the people of our time.

He celebrated 147 beatification ceremonies during which he proclaimed 1,338 Blesseds; and 51 canonisations for a total of 482 saints.

He considerably expanded the College of Cardinals, creating 231cardinals. He also called six full meetings of the College of Cardinals.

He organised 15 Assemblies of the Synod of Bishops – six Ordinary General Assemblies (1980, 1983, 1987, 1990, 1994 and 2001), one Extraordinary General Assembly (1985) and eight Special Assemblies (1980, 1991, 1994, 1995, 1997, 1998 (2) and 1999).

His most important documents include 14 Encyclicals, 15 Apostolic Exhortations, 11 Apostolic Constitutions, 45 Apostolic Letters.

Pope John Paul II appears on the balcony of St. Peter's Basilica after being elected pope on October 16, 1978. Chosen as the 263rd successor to St. Peter, Polish Cardinal Karol Wojtyla became the first non-Italian pontiff in 455 years

He promulgated the Catechism of the Catholic Church in the light of Tradition as authoritatively interpreted by the Second Vatican Council. He also reformed the Eastern and Western Codes of Canon Law, created new Institutions and reorganised the Roman Curia.

As a private Doctor he also published five books of his own: "Crossing the Threshold of Hope" (October 1994), "Gift and Mystery, on the fiftieth anniversary of my ordination as priest" (November 1996), "Roman Triptych" poetic meditations (March 2003), "Arise, Let us Be Going" (May 2004) and "Memory and Identity" (February 2005).

On April 2, 2005, at 9.37pm, while Saturday was drawing to a close and the Lord's Day was already beginning, the Octave of Easter and Divine Mercy Sunday, the Church's beloved pastor, John Paul II, departed this world.

From that evening until April 8, date of the funeral of the late Pontiff, more than three million pilgrims came to Rome to pay homage to the mortal remains of the Pope. Some of them queued up to 24 hours to enter St Peter's Basilica.

On April 28, Pope Benedict XVI announced that the normal five-year waiting period before beginning the cause of beatification and canonisation would be waived for John Paul II. The cause was officially opened by Cardinal Camillo Ruini, vicar general for the diocese of Rome, on June 28 2005.

POPE JOHN PAUL II
PONTIFICATE OCTOBER 16, 1978 TO APRIL 2, 2005

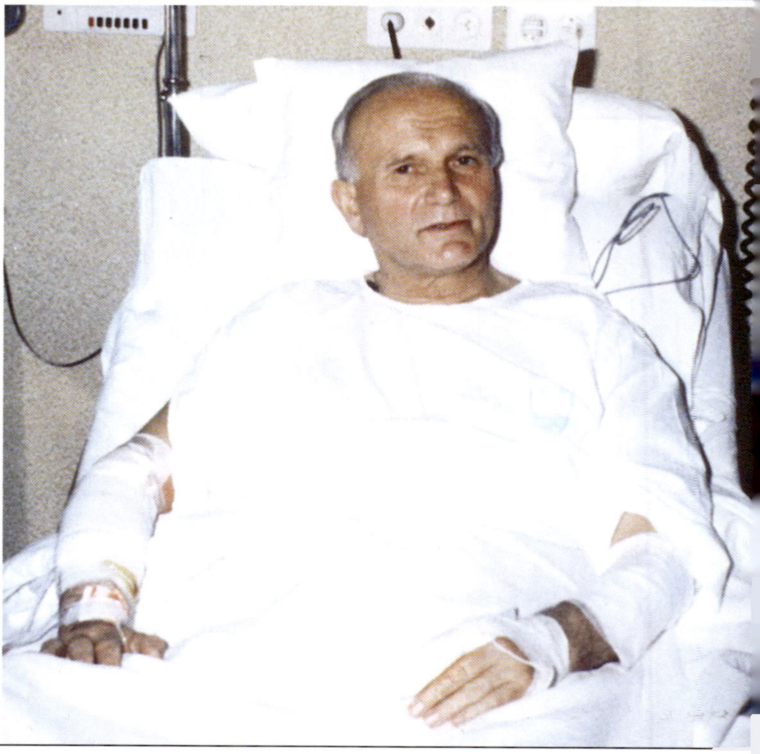

WEDNESDAY MAY 13TH 1981 WAS ONE OF THOSE GLORIOUS ROMAN SPRING DAYS, AND THE CROWDS IN ST PETER'S SQUARE WERE AT CAPACITY FOR THE WEEKLY AUDIENCE WITH THE POPE. PILGRIMS, TOURISTS, VISITING OFFICIALS, SCHOOL PARTIES, A GROUP OF POLISH PILGRIMS, BELIEVERS AND UNBELIEVERS, LAITY AND CLERGY, ALL WAITED EXPECTANTLY FOR A GLIMPSE AND A BLESSING FROM THE HOLY FATHER.

However danger lurked among the crowd, where, unnoticed, was a 23 year old Turkish assassin, Mehmet Ali Agca, a trained expert gunman who was a member of the militant group Grey Wolves, who had once before threatened to kill the pope. In fact the Turkish authorities had earlier warned the Vatican, that Agca was in Italy, possibly stalking his prey.

At 5 pm Pope John Paul II was driven into the square in his pope-mobile. The crowd as usual cheered wildly and loudly, so loudly that at 5.19 pm when shots rang out, they could scarcely be heard. The gunman had used a Browning 9-mm semiautomatic pistol, striking the pope in the stomach and perforating his colon and small intestine multiple times.

John Paul collapsed backwards into the arms of his personal secretary Father, later Cardinal, Stanisław Dziwisz. Blood spurted from his white cassock. John Paul II was rushed into the Vatican complex, and then to the Gemelli Hospital. En route to the hospital, he lost consciousness. Despite the fact that the bullets missed his mesenteric artery and abdominal aorta, he lost nearly three-quarters of his blood and neared exsanguination. He underwent five hours of surgery to treat his massive blood loss and abdominal wounds. When he briefly gained consciousness before being operated on he instructed the doctors not to remove his Brown Scapular during the operation.

The pope stated that Our Lady of Fátima helped keep him alive throughout his ordeal.

"Could I forget that the event [Ali Agca's assassination attempt] in St. Peter's Square took place on the day and at the hour when the first appearance of the Mother of Christ to the poor little peasants has been remembered for over sixty years at Fatima, Portugal? For in everything that happened to me on that very day, I felt that extraordinary motherly protection and care, which turned out to be stronger than the deadly bullet."

— Pope John Paul II -Memory & Identity, Weidenfeld & Nicolson, 2005, p.184

Agca was caught and restrained by a nun and other bystanders until police arrived. All over the world millions prayed inside and outside of churches for the Holy Father's recovery. The prayers were answered and nine days later the pope was able to broadcast from his hospital bed, in his message he forgave his would- be- assassin, "I pray for that brother of ours who shot me," he said, "and I have sincerely forgiven him."

Agca was eventually sentenced to life imprisonment. Two days after Christmas in 1983, John Paul II visited the prison where he was being held. The two spoke privately for 20 minutes. John Paul II said, "What we talked about will have to remain a secret between him and me. I spoke to him as a brother whom I have pardoned and who has my complete trust."

POPE JOHN PAUL II
PONTIFICATE OCTOBER 16, 1978 TO APRIL 2, 2005

POPE SAYS HE WILL ALLOW JPII'S SAINTHOOD CAUSE TO OPEN IMMEDIATELY

POPE BENEDICT MADE THE ANNOUNCEMENT THAT HE WAS ALLOWING THE IMMEDIATE OPENING OF **POPE JOHN PAUL II**'S CAUSE FOR SAINTHOOD, SETTING ASIDE THE FIVE-YEAR WAITING PERIOD CALLED FOR BY CHURCH LAW AT THE END OF A SPEECH TO THE PRIESTS OF THE DIOCESE OF ROME GATHERED FOR A MEETING AND A DIALOGUE WITH HIM AT THE BASILICA OF ST. JOHN LATERAN.

Pope Benedict XVI meets with priests from the Diocese of Rome at the Basilica of St. John Lateran (May 13, 2005). At the end of his prepared speech, the Pope announced that he was waiving the normal five-year waiting period for the sainthood cause of Pope John Paul II

Finishing his prepared speech to the priests, the pope said he had a "joyful announcement" to make before he listened to the priests' comments and questions.

He then read, in Latin, a letter from Cardinal Jose Saraiva Martins, prefect of the Congregation for Saints' Causes, to Cardinal Camillo Ruini, papal vicar of Rome.

The letter said that at an April 28 audience, Pope Benedict, "considering the special circumstances that were explained," had decided "to dispense from the five-year period of waiting after the death of the servant of God, Pope John Paul II ..."

Pope Benedict had to wait several minutes to finish the sentence – saying he was authorising the immediate opening of the "cause for beatification and canonisation" – because the priests broke into a loud and sustained standing ovation.

When they were quiet, he said, "I see you all understand Latin very well." The comment brought more applause.

Although the process for considering the holiness of Pope John Paul was to begin immediately, it was not expected to conclude quickly.

Even after the normal five-year waiting period, causes for beatification and canonisation require years, if not decades of studying the person's life, writings and relationships.

> **"Even after the normal five-year waiting period, causes for beatification and canonisation require years, if not decades of studying the person's life, writings and relationships."**

Those who knew the candidate are interviewed, and everything the person wrote must be scrutinised, a process that may take years, especially for a pope who was a prolific writer and speaker.

Two years after the 1997 death of Mother Teresa of Calcutta, Pope John Paul set aside the five-year waiting period for the opening of her cause, but she was not beatified until 2003.

Jesuit Father Paolo Molinari – who helped prepare her cause and is working on the cause of Pope Paul VI, who died in 1978 – said the process for a pope entails much more work.

"If this is done properly, it will take years," he said.

Pope John Paul beatified Popes Pius IX and John XXIII in 2000 – 122 and 37 years, respectively, after their deaths.

Just the interview with the Pope's longtime personal secretary, Archbishop Stanislaw Dziwisz, "will take days," Father Molinari said.

A pilgrim follows the programme at an evening prayer service in Rome which opened the cause for the beatification and canonisation of Pope John Paul II

Then there are hundreds of other people, collaborators in the Roman Curia, longtime friends, bishops and priests, who also must be interviewed. >76

POPE JOHN PAUL II
PONTIFICATE OCTOBER 16, 1978 TO APRIL 2, 2005

Thousands of Poles, some waving their national flag, attend the funeral Mass in St. Peter's Square for Pope John Paul II at the Vatican, (April 8, 2005), in Vatican City. Other pilgrims held up signs that read SANTO SUBITO which means Saint quickly, in reference to people wanting him to be made a saint as soon as possible

His published work will be examined, but also letters, articles and poems held in archives in Poland and in other parts of the world, Fr. Molinari said.

The material must be compiled into a multivolume biography, then a 'positio' or position paper on how the candidate heroically lived the Christian virtues is written.

Historians and theologians examine the material and make recommendations to members of the Congregation for Saints' Causes, whose opinion is presented to the Pope.

After the Pope declares a candidate lived a life of heroic virtue, beatification still requires the verification of a miracle attributed to his intercession.

Separate boards of theologians and of physicians are called to examine miracles alleged to have occurred after the candidate's death.

Fr. Molinari said that when Pope Benedict decided he would preside only over canonisation ceremonies – leaving Cardinal Saraiva Martins to celebrate beatification Masses – "he made it clear that he was not simplifying the process for beatification."

The Jesuit said he was not surprised the Pope set aside the waiting period because of the widespread public acclaim

of Pope John Paul's holiness and because of Pope Benedict's long relationship with him.

"He has been a faithful servant of John Paul II. He had a personal relationship with him and admiration for him," Fr. Molinari said.

During Pope John Paul's funeral, people held up signs and banners proclaiming the late pope a saint or calling for his canonisation.

Cardinal Saraiva Martins said that while popular recognition of holiness was important, 'canonical recognition' that someone is a saint requires the certainty that comes from a process developed and refined over the years.

Italian Cardinal Camillo Ruini signs a document opening the process of beatification and canonisation for Pope John Paul II in Rome (June 28, 2005)

POPE JOHN PAUL II
PONTIFICATE OCTOBER 16, 1978 TO APRIL 2, 2005

Polish Msgr. Slawomir Oder, postulator for the sainthood cause of Pope John Paul II

Sister Marie-Simon-Pierre, a member of the Little Sisters of Catholic Motherhood, poses for a photo in Aix-en-Provence, France, March 30, 2007

GRAPHOLOGIST CALLED AS WITNESS FOR LATE POPE'S SAINTHOOD CAUSE

In connection with the sainthood cause of Pope John Paul II, a graphologist and a psychiatrist were called as expert witnesses in the investigation into the presumed healing of a nun suffering from Parkinson's disease.

Msgr. Slawomir Oder, the postulator of Pope John Paul's cause, said the French diocese where the nun lives concluded its investigation and handed all its documentation to the Congregation for Saints' Causes in early April.

Msgr. Oder spoke to reporters on 27 March about the status of the cause and plans for the formal conclusion of the Rome diocesan phase of the process at the second anniversary of Pope John Paul's death.

The postulator said the French nun, whose identity had not yet been revealed, would participate in the April 2 prayer service and attend the memorial Mass Pope Benedict XVI would celebrate in St. Peter's Basilica in the evening. (The nun's name was revealed as Sr. Marie Pierre Simon).

He said the French investigation into Sr. Marie's healing was conducted "with maximum seriousness ... and a bit of the French critical attitude, which is quite useful for this kind of procedure."

The proposal to recognise that Sr. Marie was healed spontaneously and completely of Parkinson's disease – the same disease that afflicted Pope John Paul – was strengthened by the critical approach the French took, he said.

In addition to interviewing the nun, her superiors and her physicians, he said, the French diocese also had her undergo a psychiatric evaluation and had a graphologist examine samples of things she had written by hand immediately before and after the alleged healing (June 2, 2005).

One of the indicators physicians use to determine the progression of >80

POPE JOHN PAUL II
PONTIFICATE OCTOBER 16, 1978 TO APRIL 2, 2005

A worker seals boxes of documents after a Mass marking the conclusion of the initial phase of the process for the canonisation of Pope John Paul II

Parkinson's disease, he said, is the deterioration of a patient's handwriting.

"I had the opportunity to see these documents and it was amazing. It was amazing, for example, to see the last document written before that event that changed the sister's life."

The last document was "a kind of plea" for help, he said. She simply wrote, "John Paul II" in French, but it "is practically illegible. Illegible," he said.

The second document is the account she wrote the next morning about what had happened. "It is similar to the handwriting she had before the appearance of the first symptoms of Parkinson's disease."

The psychiatric evaluation "was one of the most difficult aspects of this procedure," Msgr. Oder said, and is something not usually requested as part of the procedure to verify a miracle.

"The sister was fantastic in cooperating, even though she said it was a very difficult moment for her," he said, but the diocese wanted to be sure that the improvement in her condition could not be attributed to her mental state.

The April 2 conclusion of the Rome diocesan portion of Pope John Paul's cause does not mean the process is nearing completion. The Rome Diocese will give the Vatican the testimony collected from more than 120 people who knew the Pope in Poland and in Rome, a theological evaluation of his published works that did not involve an exercise of his papal ministry and a review of unpublished written materials, including letters and retreat talks, Msgr. Oder said.

The postulator still has to compile the multi-volume 'positio,' or position paper, outlining how Pope John Paul heroically lived the Christian virtues.

While Pope Benedict set aside the normal five-year waiting period before the canonisation process could begin, even the diocesan phase and the investigation of a possible miracle were completed in almost record time, said Msgr. Mauro Parmeggiani, secretary-general of the Vicariate of Rome.

Msgr. Oder added, "The rapidity does not mean a lack of seriousness."

Msgr. Parmeggiani told reporters that with the exception of "the dispensation of the waiting period for the opening of the process, in this procedure no other dispensation was given. The entire procedure has been and is taking place with strict observance of all canonical norms."

Msgr. Oder said that on a personal level he shared the hope of many people that Pope John Paul would soon be declared a saint, "but the Church has its traditions and juridical processes" and he expects those to continue normally.

Cardinal Stanislaw Dziwisz of Krakow, Poland, prays at Pope John Paul II's tomb in the crypt under St. Peter's Basilica at the Vatican (April 2, 2007), the anniversary of the Polish pope's death. Cardinal Dziwisz served as Pope John Paul's personal secretary for nearly 40 years